CHRISTIAN PRIORITIES

CHRISTIAN PRIORITIES

by
DONALD COGGAN
Archbishop of York

LUTTERWORTH PRESS
LONDON

First published 1963

Copyright © 1963 *Donald Coggan*

Lutterworth Press
4 Bouverie Street
London, E.C.4

Harper and Row
49 East 33rd Street
New York, U.S.A.

PRINTED IN GREAT BRITAIN
BY EBENEZER BAYLIS AND SON, LTD.
THE TRINITY PRESS, WORCESTER, AND LONDON

To Jean—
dear fellow-worker in London, Toronto,
Northwood, Bradford and York

Contents

Foreword

THIS much can be said for the sermons, lectures and articles which comprise this book—they never asked to be published in book form. Nor did their author ever plan so exalted a destiny for them. But a request was made, with considerable urgency, that a collection of sermons and addresses should be made available in a more permanent form than the spoken word or the issue of a paper or journal allows. I have acceded to the request, though with a considerable measure of diffidence.

The chapters of this book reflect some major concerns which have exercised my mind and heart in recent years and which have found expression in a variety of ways. This will account for a certain element of repetition within this book, though not, I think, a very large one. A variety of style may be traced to the variety of circumstances which gave rise to the different chapters. For example, the broadcast addresses retain the informality which is necessary in using this medium of communication.

In releasing this book, I can but pray that it may help some servants of God to fasten their attention on some of the great issues facing the Church of Christ to-day, and that, as they face them in His light, they may see light.

DONALD EBOR:

Bishopthorpe
York

Acknowledgements

My thanks are due to the following publishers and owners of copyright for their kindness in giving permission to reprint articles, sermons, etc.:

Messrs. A. R. Mowbray & Co. Ltd. for No. 9, which appeared in *Lenten Counsellors*, and also to *Morehouse-Barlow Co.* who published this book in the U.S.A. under the title *These Forty Days*.

The Sunday Telegraph for No. 14, which appeared on December 24, 1961.

The Times for No. 15, published in the Supplement on the Bible in English, March 27, 1961.

The Expository Times for No. 17, published in August, 1961.

The Church of England Newspaper for No. 18, published on November 25, 1960.

The Church Times for No. 19, which appeared on November 24, 1961.

Messrs. Gard, Lyell, Bridgman & Co., 4 College Hill, Cannon Street, London, E.C.4, on behalf of the Executors of the late E. M. Butler, for permission to quote from the hymn "Lift up your hearts".

Messrs. H. Freeman & Co., 95a St. George's Road, Brighton, for permission to quote from the hymn "My God, my Father, make me strong", by Frederick Mann.

I

PRIORITIES

Necessity is laid upon me; yea, woe is unto me if I preach not the Gospel (1 Corinthians 9: 16)

An Enthronement sermon preached in York Minster, September 13, 1961, on becoming Archbishop of York

I

I CHOOSE THESE phrases as my text to-day, partly because the closing words constitute the text which, in its Latin form, is engraved on the pectoral cross given me by my students at the time of my consecration as a bishop. They are, therefore, words which hold a very special significance for me. I choose them, also, because they come from the writings of one whose life and thought have been formative for me down the years. But I choose them also because they summarize with extraordinary precision and clarity the task of the Christian Church, a task which never changes, however much the particular contemporary situation may vary from age to age.

The words presuppose, on the part of the Apostle, a life of worship and prayer. This First Epistle to the Corinthians, indeed, deals with these matters in relation to the sacrament of Holy Communion in particular; and behind all the Epistles of St. Paul we can see the figure of a man whose devotional life was such that, in private prayer and corporate worship, he knew what it was to live in touch with the Most High. Every generation has to learn afresh that activity apart from worship, organization divorced from prayer, life without communion with God, is fatuous, so much

sound and fury, signifying nothing.

That is not pious talk. It is hard, down-to-earth fact.

Here in this text, however, the Apostle's glance is not vertical but horizontal. He was concerned with the world around him, in relation to the Gospel of Christ. That Gospel he regarded as a treasure of the most priceless value. As he pondered it, he felt a kind of awed surprise that God should have allowed him to preach the unsearchable riches of Christ. It was miracle—he, the least of all saints, put in trust with *this*! So he looked out over his world. It was a world in which an uneasy peace reigned under the sovereignty of a semi-despotic, semi-kindly Roman power. It was a world in which the Christian forces were the tiniest minority movement, whose message was to the Jews a stumbling-block and to the intellectuals a good joke. But that was neither here nor there. He had been entrusted with the Good News of God's advent among men in Christ; of the great saving acts of history centred in Jesus; and necessity was laid upon him—"yea, woe is unto me if I preach not the Gospel."

There are parallels between the world of St. Paul's day and our own. If we had time, we might trace many such parallels— the uneasy peace, the mania for pleasure, the desire for security, the cynicism of an age which was losing its grip on the old faiths and had not yet grasped a new one adequate for its needs. That would be an interesting historical exercise. But it is not our task to-day. Rather, we should do well to look again at the Christian Gospel, and ask whether the Church is preaching that Gospel in a way relevant to the world of the 1960's. And when I say the Church, I do not mean simply the clergy in their pulpits, but the *Church*—men and women, clerical and lay, who are irrevocably committed to Christ their Lord, committed to the doing of His will, to the fighting of His battles and to the propagation of His Faith.

The tragedy within the Church to-day, all too often, is that the Gospel that is preached is but a section, a fragment, of the Gospel as it is given to us in the New Testament. We are children of our generation, and we are beset by the limitations of our generation. Sixty years ago one might imagine, from many of the hymns sung, that Christianity had little concern with the things of everyday life, but only a consuming interest in the world to come. That is clearly a travesty of the Christian Faith, whose Founder spent much of His public ministry in healing bowed bodies and twisted minds, and who was desperately concerned with the sheer physical needs of the people whom He met day by day.

Now, on the other hand, unless I am very much mistaken, we have swung too much the other way. We all have to die. However much our lives may differ here, we all have that in common. We shall all stand before the judgment seat of Christ.

16

One of the tasks of the Christian Church is to teach me how to die, as well as how to live; to teach me the bright hope of resurrection life in Christ both here and now, and there and then. And if one is emphasized or stressed to the neglect of the other, then to that degree a travesty of the Christian Gospel is presented. But when a Gospel is declared which is at once intimately personal and compassionately social in its implications; which is as earthy and materialistic as was the Incarnation itself; and which is at the same time concerned with the Life of the world to come—then we have a message adequate for us men who have to live out our years in the hurly-burly of a twentieth-century civilization, and who are destined to reach our fulfilment as the sons of God in the world beyond. I must have a Gospel adequate for *this* life and for *that*. Woe to the Church if she preaches not such a Gospel!

Again, it is possible to preach a pseudo-Gospel or to embrace a pseudo-Christian Faith, which is no wider in its interest than the confines of our own parish, or of our own race. If ever the folly of that viewpoint was apparent, it is so to-day. The world is on our doorstep, whether we like it or not. Colour-bar and race distinction make no sense when the implications of the Gospel are considered. "Christ died for all"; hence all are equally dear to God. We can, therefore, think no longer in terms of overseas missions as over against the work of the Church at home. This is one work, as there is one Lord and one faith and one baptism. It is much more important that the Christian task should be got on with in Africa than that my parish church should have a new luxury organ. It is urgent that Indian Christians should be adequately trained as doctors, clergy and teachers, so as to meet the challenge of a new age; and that the Church should make her voice heard and her influence felt to help the three to five hundred million people who go hungry even in normal times, even though this means sacrifice and a new pattern of Church life here.

This is the ordinary, humdrum, yet thrilling work of the Church. It is not the job of a few enthusiasts in each parish. To share vigorously in the missionary work of the Church is the bounden duty—as it is the high privilege—of every dedicated Christian. *"Go forth into the world . . ."* says the bishop at the end of the Confirmation service, echoing the last command of the Church's Lord. "Go forth . . ." Push on, and out, and forward. Into the homes and factories and streets of England—I would like to see a revival of open-air witness here at home, in spite of the difficulties of modern traffic. Into the lands where the younger Churches are still very young, and under-staffed and inexperienced, and where there is still great need of those who have skills which they are prepared to use as servants of the local Christians. Into the lands where Christ's Cross has as yet not been firmly planted, and where broken bodies and minds and unlit souls need the Gospel. *"Go forth."* A confirmed Christian who has no missionary passion is not worthy of his commission by the Head of the Church.

I have spoken, first, of a Gospel large enough for men's needs in this world and the next; and, secondly, of a Gospel for all races and nations and kindreds and tongues.

If such a Gospel is to be proclaimed by us clergy and laity in this our generation, what particular word has God to say to us as we put our hands to the task? Very humbly I would suggest two things:

I. *We need a fresh awareness of God the Holy Spirit.*

It is in and through the Body of Christ that the Holy Spirit moves and works. But what if the members of that Body are deaf, their minds stagnant, or their wills lethargic? What if they are so set in their ways that they are not prepared for risk and venture? The Holy Spirit is spoken of as wind and fire—and these are uncomfortable elements. What if the Holy Spirit is seeking to move us into untravelled paths, to shew us the unexpected in the realm of reunion, to challenge us to trust Him and to experiment as we have not dared to do before if that is the cost of ending the scandal of disunity? "Come as the wind . . . Come as the fire . . ." So we pray. What if God answered that prayer in unforeseen and unusual ways at your next Parochial Church Council meeting, or at the next gathering of Convocation or Church Assembly? Should we be prepared to go forward? Or would fear or over-caution hold us back?

II. *We need a fresh understanding of the Bible.*

Our generation is the generation of new translations. Thank God for that. Bible circulation is higher than ever before. That is all to the good. But no one in his wildest moments of optimism would say that the England of Queen Elizabeth II's day "is the people of a book and that book the Bible", as it was said of the people of the reign of Queen Elizabeth I. One result of that sad fact can be seen in the record of crime and of moral lapse which is ours. It is nothing to be proud of.

What is to be done? I believe it is for the Church to get its priorities right here again; to take a fresh look at its programme of activities; to see whether, year by year, a fresh supply of men and women is being produced who know their Faith and why they hold it, and who can put that Faith across in simple terms relevant to the situation in which they earn their living. Many organizations which now occupy much time and energy in our churches could well die a comely death! This activity of producing intelligent Christians with an infectious faith is at once one of the main reasons for the existence of the Church, and one of the most clamant needs of the world.

We began with St. Paul—"Necessity is laid upon me; yea, woe is unto me if I preach not the Gospel." We end with Simon Peter, whose name this great shrine of York bears. "Simon, son of Jonas, lovest thou Me?" These were the words of the Risen Christ. "Yea, Lord, Thou knowest that I love Thee." That was St. Peter's answer. It is when that answer goes up from the followers of the Crucified in all reality that the Church begins once again to get her priorities right, to see the fulness of her task, and, in eager submission to that Holy Spirit who is wind and fire, to prosecute that task "till He come".

Let the word go out to every Christian soul in this building, and to every Christian soul listening-in far beyond this Minster —"*Back* to the Love of Jesus our Lord; *forward* to a new obedience to the Holy Spirit; *out* to a needy world in pity and compassion. Soldiers of Christ, arise, and put your armour on!"

2

"*TAKE CARE OF THE CHURCH OF GOD*"

He fed them with a faithful and true heart, and ruled them prudently with all his power (Psalm 78:73, Prayer Book Version)

An Enthronement sermon preached in Bradford Cathedral, February 3, 1956, on becoming Bishop of Bradford

2

N O ONE, UNLESS he were completely devoid of a sense of history, could take part in the ceremonies connected with the consecration and enthronement of a bishop in the Church of God without being deeply moved. No one, unless he were blind to the march of events, could fail at least to catch a glimpse of the particular significance at this time of these services in which so many of us have participated in York and in this Cathedral Church of Bradford. We have been caught up into the stream of history. We have taken our share in the re-enactment of those rites by which God guides and governs His Church. And we have felt ourselves to be—as indeed we are—part of that great Church which goes on from generation to generation, from century to century, and which is imperishable, for it is the Body of Christ Himself.

I have alluded to the particular significance *at this time* of those events in which we have shared. I believe that this is a most thrilling time to have a part in the work of the Church of Christ. I cannot align myself with those who, wistfully looking back to the Victorian era or to some other by-gone age, dismally hanker for "the good old days". "*This* is the day which the Lord hath made; we will rejoice and be glad in it." "*Now* is the accepted time, behold *now* is the day of salvation."

That there are difficulties facing the Church, that there are enemies rampant, that there are problems abundant—these things are so obvious that they scarcely need to be stated. But I believe it is clear, to those who have eyes to see, that the Hand of God is powerfully at work in our country. Something of that old lethargy which marred the work of the Church, and the old apathy which strangled the spiritual life of the nation in the thirties and early forties of this century, is beginning to pass. Slowly men are coming to see that they cannot live by bread alone. Gradually it is beginning to dawn on them that man needs more than food and housing, more even than education

23

and secular culture, if he is to live as a son of the Most High God. He may not be able to analyse his need, to diagnose his deep spiritual sickness. If he could he would say with the Psalmist "My soul is athirst for GOD, even for the living God." But needy he is—and that need constitutes to-day's great challenge to the Church.

It was to me a wonderful experience to realize that the best part of 2,000 people travelled from this diocese to York to share in the Consecration service of one who, to most of them, was a stranger. It seemed to me to be an indication of a Church life which, to put it mildly, is by no means dead in this part of Yorkshire. I have watched, with a kind of fascinated interest, the response of this great city and diocese to the appeal for the enlargement and glorification of its Mother Church. Men do not give £170,000 in some three months to a cause for which they have little concern. And—far more significant than any figures or finances can ever be—I have been moved by the devotion of those who, during the time since the last Bishop retired and also during the months of his illness, have worked unsparingly for the welfare of the life of the Church.

Those of you who know God at first hand will understand what I mean when I say that often, and particularly at times of crisis, a Biblical sentence or phrase suddenly becomes luminous to them. They may have read it scores of times before. They may have pondered it previously. But, so far, it has had no special meaning for them, no sense of authoritative significance. Then, in an hour big with grave decision, it becomes to them a very Word of God. The day after I was first approached in regard to the acceptance of the bishopric of this diocese, I was sitting in my accustomed seat in my College Chapel. The second Lesson was from the 3rd Chapter of the 1st Epistle to Timothy. In that chapter the office and work of a bishop is described. One phrase stood out, luminous, from the rest of the passage—"take care of the Church of God". I found that the original phrase "take care" occurs but once else in the New Testament, in that parable of Jesus in which He described how the Samaritan "took care" of the man who fell among thieves on the road to Jericho, and how he charged the innkeeper, during his own absence, to "take care" of him till he should

24

return. As I pondered on this, I said to myself: "Is not this the primary function of the bishop in the Church of God?—to take care of the Body, broken and rent as it may be, and to see that that Body fulfils the function in society which is in the Mind of God for it?"

I have chosen as my text for to-day the words of the closing verse of the 78th Psalm. I have quoted them in the form in which they occur in our Prayer Book Version, not necessarily because that is the most accurate rendering of the original but because that version expresses the ideal of episcopacy as it presents itself to me. "He fed them with a faithful and true heart, and ruled them prudently with all his power." There you have it—the picture, with all its delicate shades and half-tones, of the Shepherd King David. But you have more. You have the almost perfect delineation of a bishop as he should be—over-shepherd (yet always under "that great Shepherd of the Sheep", Jesus our Lord); tenderness and sacrifice combined in that great simile; authority and government hinted at in the words "ruling them prudently with all his power". An impossible ideal? Yes—utterly and absolutely impossible—but for the grace of God and the prayers, the constant, urgent, upholding prayers of his people, not only on the day of his Enthronization but on the long and sometimes weary days of routine work ahead.

On the Feast of the Conversion of Saint Paul in York Minster 35 years ago, William Temple was consecrated Bishop in the Church of God. Three weeks later he was enthroned as Bishop of Manchester. His biographer tells us that on that occasion Temple spoke these simple and memorable words:

> I come as a learner, with no policy to advocate, no plan already formed to follow. But I come with one burning desire; it is that in all our activities, sacred and secular, ecclesiastical and social, we should help each other to fix our eyes on Jesus, making Him our only guide . . . Pray for me, I ask you, not chiefly that I may be wise and strong, or any other such thing, though for these things I need your prayers. But pray for me chiefly that *I may never let go of the unseen hand of the Lord Jesus and may live in daily fellowship with Him.* It is so that you will most of all help me to help you. So shall we go forward together—not without stumbling, not without

weariness, but always towards the loving welcome that awaits us in our Father's home, where the conflicts which now beset the earth will have vanished, where self-seeking cannot find entrance, where misery gives place to joy and quarrelling to peace, because self is either sacrificed or forgotten in the realization of the Love of God.

Those words I would make my own on this day of my coming among you. Already I have seen enough to know that many problems await us, that many decisions must soon be made, that swift action is called for in many realms. Where possible that action will be taken quickly. Where it seems better to wait, I ask for your patience until I have been able to weigh up the situation and get to know the diocese and its people. But above all I ask, as William Temple asked, that you will pray for me "that I may never let go of the unseen hand of the Lord Jesus and may live in daily fellowship with Him". That way lies vision without which the people perish. That way lies the passion for evangelism without which the sheep are never brought home to the Good Shepherd. That way lies worship, without which the soul becomes arid and barren.

"He fed them with a faithful and true heart, and ruled them prudently with all his power." Dare I ask that you will turn that into a prayer for him who comes among you to-day, that he may in very truth "feed the flock over which the Holy Ghost has made him an overseer"?

3

THE MESSAGE OF CHRISTMAS

God so loved the world that He gave His only begotten
Son (St. John 3:16)

A sermon broadcast in the General Overseas Service of the B.B.C.,
December 23, 24, and 25, 1961

3

THERE ARE SOME things to which no one except the most blasé ever grows accustomed. They remain a source of wonder. For example—travel by air. I came back recently from India, and I travelled by jet. I had done a good deal of travel by air before, but, even so, I could not but marvel at the miracle of spending a long evening with friends in Delhi, and lunching next day in London. Or at the power of those four mighty engines which shot that huge plane up into the sky and held it there in flight as we traversed continents!

Or again—this miracle of radio, by which one man, sitting in a studio in Yorkshire, can have his words recorded, in the knowledge that in the course of the next few days they will be broadcast almost all over the world. My mind travels to friends with whom I have lived, or whom I have visited, in North and South America (especially in Toronto), in Africa East and West, in India, and elsewhere. I can picture you, and tens of thousands of others besides, who will be listening in. It would be an enormous privilege if my words might be taken by you as a message from the Old Country—and especially a message from the Church in the Old Country—which brought an assurance of affection and concern at this time. We do not forget you. We hold you in our thoughts and prayers.

But to go back to my theme of miracles and not getting accustomed to them. Air-travel. Radio. Yes; it is a pity to get blasé about things like these. A sense of *wonder* is good. But there is one thing to which all too many of us have grown accustomed. In fact, we hardly give it a thought—the central event of Christmas. Notice, will you, just how I put that. I said, "the central event". For, of course, to millions of us Christmas means family reunions, and turkey, and champagne, and presents, and a tree lit up and loaded; and for some of us it means snow, and for others of us, in Australia and elsewhere, heat. To some of us, there may be passing allusions on the Christmas cards to "peace

29

on earth and goodwill among men"; but it amounts to little.
And the angels and all that which form part of the decorations
mean little more than Father Christmas and the reindeer.
But all these things are the trappings—good trappings, good
fun, but trappings none the less! I am talking about the central
event of Christmas—and it is this which so easily gets forgotten,
and it is this which so easily we get accustomed to, and about
which we get blasé.

Dorothy Sayers, as all the world knows, was a great writer of
detective stories. Not everybody knows, however, that she was
also a great writer on the Christian Faith. Her book, *The
Mind of the Maker*, for example, is well worth reading. Some
years back, she wrote a little book called *The Greatest Drama
Ever Staged*. In it she dealt with the kind of thing I am speaking
about to-day—about getting so accustomed to the "old, old
story" that we cease to wonder at it, and even reach the point
where we hardly give it a thought. In fact, about thinking of the
Christian message as "dull". She breaks a lance with those who
dare to speak of "dull dogma":

> It is [she writes] the neglect of dogma that makes for dullness.
> The Christian faith is the most exciting drama that ever staggered
> the imagination of man—and the dogma *is* the drama. That
> drama is summarized quite clearly in the creeds of the Church,
> and if we find it dull it is because we either have never really read
> those amazing documents, or have recited them so often and so
> mechanically as to have lost all sense of their meaning.

Then, in her own stark language, she outlines what she calls

> the tale of the time when God was the under-dog and got beaten,
> when He submitted to the conditions He had laid down and
> became a man like the men He had made, and the men He had
> made broke Him and killed Him. This is the dogma we find so
> dull—this terrifying drama of which God is the victim and hero.
> If this is dull, then what, in Heaven's name, is worthy to be called
> exciting?

She is right, you know; she is dead right. And the essence of
my Christmas message to you is this—to ask you to break free,
for a spell this year, from the trappings, and to take a steady

look at the central event and at its meaning for you and the world you live in. "God so loved the world that He gave His only begotten Son." Think of what that means. It means, to begin with, that He loved *you*, and that His Son gave Himself for *you*. It is as personal and intimate as that. It does not say that He *will* love you if you are good and worthy of His love. It says that He loves you as you are—even if you are in despair of yourself and have forfeited the love of those nearest and dearest to you. *Such* is the love of God for you. And that He loves the *world* means that there is no one outside the sphere and scope of God's care. He loves them, whether they belong to East or West, whether they are conservative or communist, whether their colour is black or white—*all* are dear to Him, inasmuch as Christ thought all precious enough to die for them. The implications of that are, of course, shattering.

When I was in Delhi, I made a point of walking round the old city one afternoon for a couple of hours. There, in close proximity to the wealthy city of New Delhi, I saw the almost hopeless plight of thousands of poverty-stricken, illiterate Indians, many of them with nothing but an old rag between them and the pavement every night. If I believe that Christ died for them quite as much as He did for me, then I am bound to be swept up into a great care, a costly care for the homeless, the illiterate, the under-privileged. And if I believe the black man is as dear to God as the white man, I must treat him with the same respect as I would treat myself or any fellow white man. Uncomfortable dogma? Undoubtedly. Dull dogma? Undoubtedly *not*, for it impinges directly on mind and will and action!

Look again at the Christmas story. Here is One whom St. John calls "the Word", that is to say, the very heart and mind of God disclosed for men to see and handle. "The Word, and yet unable to speak a word"—so Launcelot Andrewes described the impotence of the Babe of Bethlehem. Look at the stable, not through the eyes of a mediaeval artist whose colours make angels, eastern kings, and even animals, glitter with glory; but through the eyes of a realism which sees the pathos of a pregnant woman with nowhere but a stinking stable in which to give birth to her Son. And watch that little Son taken, soon

31

after His birth, as a refugee to Egypt, there to be safe from the wrath of the dictator-king. This is what is involved when we speak of God becoming man, of God loving man. And it is but a prelude to a life in which He refused the way of power and accepted the way of suffering. So people said of the Christ: "Himself bore our griefs, and carried our sorrows." He did—right up to the day when He carried our sins to the tree.

I suppose the real trouble is that we confuse love with sentimentality, and that is why we get blasé about Christianity, and even bored with it. For sentimentality is a sickly thing. A dash of it now and then may not do much harm. But too much of it is nauseating. Not so with love. Love is a great, strong, muscular thing. Love, as the Bible shows it to us, has to do with the rescue of men and women and children from everything which makes life rotten and flabby—from self-centredness, and self-indulgence, from all that is impure and unclean. That was the Love that "came down at Christmas". "Came down" for us men and for our salvation. "Came down", and got all mixed up with the problems created by our sin and selfishness. Love—of *that* quality—can never be uninteresting, for it is so close to life, life as it is all around us, life in the raw. Love is concerned, deeply concerned, with things like the mess some people are making of their marriages; with the selfishness which results in millions of pounds every year being spent on cosmetics and drink, while the agencies which look after refugees have to make do on a shoe-string. Love is concerned with the fact that tens of millions of people will go hungry this Christmas season, while we have heaps to eat. It is concerned with the fact that while we are so accustomed to the privilege of having books and being able to read them that we will hardly go round the corner to buy a copy of the new translation of the Bible, millions of adults in Africa still cannot read. Love is concerned with the homeless, with the refugee, with the leper (two millions of them in India alone!), with the Christless. Love is like that. And if *we* are not concerned about these people with a costly concern, it means that love, the love of God, has not got far into our systems. Then it is no wonder that we hardly give a thought to the Christian message—that we get blasé about it, or even bored by it.

I said at the beginning of this Christmas message that wonder was a good thing. I believe that—for it is akin to worship. Coleridge said: "The sense of worship begins as the child of wonder and becomes the father of praise." And worship takes place when you begin to face the claim of the holy love of God on you; begin to let your conscience be quickened by God's holiness; your mind be nourished by God's truth; your heart be opened to God's love—begin, in fact, to surrender your will to the purpose of God for you as an individual, as a responsible member of society, as one tiny part of the world which God loves and for which Christ died.

That, then, is my message to you wherever you may be this Christmas season. God give you His peace and joy, the peace that passes all understanding, and the joy that comes from the knowledge that you are doing His will.

4

THE MESSAGE OF EASTER

Our Saviour Jesus Christ has broken the power of death and brought life and immortality to light through the Gospel (2 Timothy 1:10, *New English Bible*)

A sermon preached in York Minster, Easter Day, 1962

4

A WIT ONCE SAID that a man's last enemy is not death, but the writer who composes his obituary notice. It was a clever remark, but in a sense a silly one; for, once a man is dead, he is out of reach of the arrows, however barbed they may be, which the obituary writer may loose at him.

It is the Christian contention, however, that death is not an ogre to be feared. It is indeed a *fact* to be faced, for there is not one among us who is exempt from meeting it. With the help of the medical profession we may postpone its advent a little. But escape it? No. It may come to us slowly, by the natural wearing out of our bodies; or it may come to us suddenly through accident or atomic war. But come it will. It is inescapable. He is a wise man who faces that fact frankly and fully, and prepares to meet it however and whenever it comes. I am pretty sure that much of the restlessness, the nervousness, the edginess of modern life is due to the fact that for very many death is a kind of skeleton in the cupboard, and we dare not face it. We camouflage it. We dress it up. We disguise it. But all the time it is there.

Easter, of all the seasons of the year, is the one which deals radically with this problem. It tells us that the prospect of death need not dismay us, if we are in Christ. For Christ, so the Easter message affirms, has broken the power of death, destroyed its potency to hurt, drawn its sting. This is an amazing claim. Let us look at it for a moment.

One of the commonest errors about Christianity is that it is a recipe for being good, that its primary purpose is to tell men how to improve themselves as life goes on. That is a great fallacy. Christianity is essentially a story—a story of what God has done about man's great enemies of sin and death; of what He, by His Spirit through His Church, is still doing in this sphere; of the climax towards which He is working and which He will finally achieve. This story is centred in the Person of

37

Jesus Christ, not so much in what He taught (though that is of immense importance), as in what He was and did. Especially clearly is that seen in the events which we connect with Good Friday and Easter Day. Here the drama of His life reached its climax. The forces of anti-God, of sin, of self-interest, of fear and of hate, did their worst. They did to death Jesus, the Christ of God. And the godless laughed and said that was the end of Jesus of Nazareth, the end of His dreams about the Kingdom of God, the denial of all that He had stood for. But they had forgotten about God. The *fool* said: "There is no God." He still does. But it doesn't make any difference to the fact. He *is*. He *reigns*. He *acts*. So He did on the first Easter Day. He raised Jesus. He vindicated the right. He broke the power of death.

This is the Christian faith in its essence. You may not like it. You may ignore it. You may deny it. But this is it. Take away the Cross and Resurrection from Christianity, and you have a poor, lifeless, maimed thing left, one more religion in the weary list of faiths which have come and gone in the centuries. On the other hand, keep the Cross and Resurrection of Jesus central to your message, as the early Christians did and as the New Testament does, and you have a Gospel adequate for men's needs, men who wrestle with sin and face the fact of death. This is a Gospel big enough for this life and for the next—and I need a Gospel of that dimension. So do you.

Look at this again. The text would have us believe that the hymn is literally correct when it avers:

> Death's mightiest powers have done their worst,
> And Jesus hath His foes dispersed—

His foes, and ours! He has broken the power of death. Before the first Good Friday and Easter Day, there were "intimations of immortality" (to borrow a phrase of Wordsworth's), hints of life beyond, but little more. But here in the Risen Christ is One who has invaded the dark domain of death as the great Pioneer, wrested from it its power, and returned, the first of a vast host of one-time captives whom He has freed from death's terrors for ever. Life and immortality are brought to light. What was hitherto hidden is now revealed. In Christ all are made alive. No wonder that the New Testament is a book jubilant. No

wonder that the Christian is a man triumphant. He has—
already—passed from death to life. Death for him will indeed
mean the physical dissolution of his body; but it will be something infinitely wonderful, for it will mean seeing face to face
the One who has redeemed and restored him, and it will mean
reunion with those in Christ who have gone before him.

Among the English poets who have dealt with this subject,
Richard Baxter must surely take a high place. This seventeenth-
century writer, in one of his poems called "The Exit", writes
with quiet confidence,

> Christ who knows all his sheep
> Will all in safety keep;
> He will not lose his blood,
>   Nor intercession:
> Nor we the purchased good
>   Of his dear Passion.

> Lord Jesus, take my spirit:
> I trust thy love and merit:
> Take home this wandering sheep,
>   For thou hast sought it:
> This soul in safety keep,
>   For thou hast bought it.

So much for his personal hope in Christ. But the Christian's
belief is not only individualistic; it is corporate also. So Baxter
writes again:

> As for my friends, they are not lost;
>   The several vessels of thy fleet,
> Though parted now, by tempest tost,
>   Shall safely in the haven meet.

> Still we are centred all in thee,
>   Members, though distant, of one Head;
> In the same family we be,
>   By the same faith and spirit led.

> Before thy throne we daily meet
>   As joint-petitioners to thee;
> In spirit we each other greet,
>   And shall again each other see.

We must look, yet again, a little deeper into this Christian hope. It is based, not on wishful thinking which longs for continuity when this little life is over. It is the consequence of the belief that God is righteous and that God is love. He made us; He loves us; He will not let us perish. A mere belief in immortality need not be a religious thing at all. It may be a purely selfish thing—*I* want to continue and *I* want to see my friends again! But "if"—as William Temple put it—"if my desire is first for God's glory, and for myself that I may be used to promote it, then the doctrine of immortality will give me new heart in the assurance that what here must be a very imperfect service may be made perfect hereafter, that my love of friends may be one more manifestation of the over-flowing Love Divine, and that God may be seen as perfect Love in the eternal fellowship of love to which He calls us."

"He that hath this hope in him," said St. John, not many decades after the first Easter Day, "purifieth himself even as He is pure." Just so. The resurrection hope, brought to us by Christ and in Christ, is a mighty ethical power. If this little life is a training ground for the next, a preparation for the day when I shall see my Lord face to face, then my whole order of priorities in the here and now will be totally different from those whose world view, whose philosophy of life is bounded by the brief span of seventy or eighty years. Response to Him who calls me out of darkness into His marvellous light; obedience to the dictates of His will for me and through me for the world; worship in the family of His people; service for the welfare of His needy ones; exploration of His ways with the children of men—these are the things which will come first. These are the things which will be seen to abide, while many things that the world holds dearest will be seen for the tinsel and the trimmings that they are.

So the Easter message comes to us once again—comes to us when men's hearts are failing them for fear, comes to us in an age of uncertainty which for many is the consequence of the abandonment of Christian beliefs. It points us back to the facts apart from which our preaching is vain and your faith is vain—that Christ is risen from the dead, that He has broken the power of death and brought life and immortality to light through the

40

Gospel. It points us forward to the day of His ultimate triumph, when He shall reign, and sorrow and sighing shall be no more. It points us to the here and now, to the rough and tumble of discipleship, to the present wrestling with sin and wrong, to the battle for the Lord to which every Christian man and woman is committed.

And so I say "Lift up your hearts".

Lift up your hearts! We lift them, Lord, to Thee;
Here at Thy feet none other may we see:
"Lift up your hearts!" E'en so, with one accord,
We lift them up, we lift them to the Lord.

Above the level of the former years,
The mire of sin, the slough of guilty fears,
The mist of doubt, the blight of love's decay,
O Lord of Light, lift all our hearts to-day!

5

THE MAKING OF SAINTS

Blessed are they that have not seen, and yet have believed
(St. John 20:29)

A sermon preached in Chester Cathedral on the occasion of the dedication
of its West Window, St. Thomas's Day, December 21, 1961

5

ONE CLEAR NOTE rings consistently through this service. One clear light shines through the great West window which it has been my high privilege to dedicate to-day. The note is that of the triumph of God's saints. The light is the radiance of Christ at work in them and through them.

This is a great theme—a theme worked out with consummate ingenuity and splendid skill in our new window. There, in steady array, stand the Twelve Apostles, and, below them, a shining galaxy of Saints, the Blessed Virgin Mary (with Child), and St. Joseph in the middle, themselves the centre of a phalanx of Saints, all of whom are associated with the vigorous life of the Church in the North of England.

On this we have looked to-day. We have pondered, as we listened to the Gospel, on the theme of St. Thomas who was by no means a ready-made saint (if such a thing there ever be!). On the contrary, there was a man who spurned a creed received at secondhand, who fought his way through doubt and difficulty to a living faith, and who, once he grasped the truth cf what he had long wanted to believe, threw himself into wholehearted discipleship, with the cry: "My Lord and my God."

"What is a saint?" said the schoolmaster to his class. "A saint," replied one of the children, "is a man the light shines through." He was thinking of the kind of thing we have been looking at to-day, the stained-glass-window saint. But did he not speak better than he knew? Did he not give us an accurate description of what, precisely, the saints have been all down the ages—*and are to-day*?

What do you think of, when the word "Saint" is spoken? I think of St. Paul, persecutor turned apostle, who down the years has been so formative, through his life and through his letters, in my own thinking. I think of St. John, apostle and mystic, with whose name is associated what may well be the

45

most profound book ever written. I think of St. Augustine who, when the Gothic hordes were sweeping down on Rome and the old Empire was breaking up in A.D. 410, wrote his *City of God*, and thus turned the eyes of a trembling people to the city which hath foundations, whose builder and architect is God. I think of those whose names are incorporated in this window—men and women who deserve the title of leaders of the Church. I think of men of a wide variety of churchmanship who, down the centuries, have left their mark and enriched the life of the Body of Christ in this land—a Lightfoot and a Westcott, a Wesley and a Newman, a Temple and a Maurice, a Wilson Carlile and a Marie Carlile. You could add to the list almost *ad infinitum*. But I think also of many a one whom I have known personally, whose names rarely, if ever, got into print, but who answered to the description of men and women through whom the light of Christ shone. I think of a little old woman in a London slum parish where I served—almost blind, almost completely deaf, living in a horrid room three storeys up, and eking out her existence on a pension of ten shillings a week. But the light shone in her and through her.

I think of a lady in my last diocese of Bradford, bed-ridden for thirteen long years, with a disease which every year left her more and more helpless. But her room was the power house of the parish. The light shone through her.

I need not go on. You see the point I am making. When you use the word "saint", you do not have to look back into ancient history, though it will do you good to do so from time to time. God is always making saints. Indeed, from one angle, the Church may be described as a factory where God does just that, using as His tools all kinds of things—Word and Sacrament, worship and prayer, suffering and discipline, joy and grief.

He wants to do that with you. No—I am not talking about the man sitting next you. I am talking about you. He wants to make you a man—a woman—through whom the light of Christ will shine, "conformed", as one of our prayers to-day put it, "conformed to the image of Thy dear Son". "Each", as another prayer phrased it, "each in his office lowly serving, till all nations confess Thy Name and all mankind know and fulfil his destiny in Christ." "That for me?" Yes, that—for you! What a calling!

Thomas saw and believed. Thomas reached hither his finger and beheld the Hands; reached hither his hand, and thrust it into the Side. We cannot do that. But we can inherit the blessing reserved for those who have never seen, and yet have believed. Of course, everything hangs on that word. Believing—faith—person to Person trust in the Christ of God, come down, as at this time, for us men and for our salvation.

I go back to this lovely window. I never mentioned the uppermost part of the window, and yet it is in many ways the most important part. Three circles represent the Holy Trinity, Father, Son and Holy Spirit. And below those three circles are flying doves, representing the sevenfold gifts of the Spirit. What does that mean in terms of the making of saints, which is the central theme of the window? It means that all the power of the Godhead is available to make men—to make me—a person through whom the Light shines. What a fool I am, if, by clinging to sin or neglecting the means of grace, I block that power, I abuse that grace!

> All power is here and round me now,
> Faithful I stand in rule and vow,
> While 'tis not I, but ever Thou:
> Thy will be done.

So the work of God goes on in the lives of men, through the power of God:

> God, whose city's sure foundation
> Stands upon His holy hill,
> By His mighty inspiration
> Chose of old *and chooseth still*
> Men of every race and nation
> His good pleasure to fulfil.

So the Light shines on in the darkness of the world. So the Light of Christ shines out through mortal men—through you, please God; and, in His infinite mercy, through me.

47

6

A SAINT IN THE MAKING

May the Lord direct your hearts towards God's love and
the steadfastness of Christ! (2 Thessalonians 3:5, *New
English Bible*)

A sermon preached in Rochester Cathedral at a Thanksgiving for the life
of Christopher Maude Chavasse (Bishop of Rochester 1940–60), on
March 24, 1962

6

THE LETTERS OF St. Paul are adorned with prayers, as a rich mantle may be studded with jewels. It was natural for the Apostle to pass from the directions of an Epistle to a prayer for those to whom he wrote. So his letter writing was transformed from a chore into a ministry. The Epistles to the Thessalonians are no exception. The text which I have chosen is one of these prayers. It has nothing to do—as the Authorized Version would suggest—with the Second Advent, "the patient waiting for Christ". It is a prayer that the Thessalonians' lives might be marked by two things—the love of God and that steadfastness, that endurance which marked the life of the Master. It is a splendid prayer. Let us pray it for one another in our various vocations—"Lord, direct our hearts into the love of God, and into the steady endurance which marked Thy ministry at every step."

This prayer was richly answered in the life of him in whose memory this great company meets to-day. I do not need to sketch in any detail the main events of the life of Christopher Maude Chavasse—the godly and happy home, the years at Oxford marked by great athletic prowess, the rough and tumble of a Lancashire curacy, the challenge of the period at St. Aldate's, Oxford, the building of the young St. Peter's Hall at Oxford, and then the twenty heavy years as Bishop of Rochester. That is known to us all. What I am concerned to do, as best I may, is to try to put my finger on the secrets that made possible the achievements which I have so briefly outlined.

The love of God, and a Christ-like endurance. Those two things get pretty close to the secret.

It was the love of God burning in him which made him so great a protagonist of evangelism in the Church. His Chairmanship of the Archbishops' Commission on Evangelism which produced the Report entitled *Towards the Conversion of England* was one of the most remarkable achievements of his life. A religious weekly may be right in referring to "one of the greatest disappointments of his life—the failure to implement on a national scale the valuable report". That may be so. But it would, I think, be true to say that it was that Report very largely which brought evangelism back into a central place in the thinking and praying of the Church, and which helped Christian people to see that evangelism is not a kind of optional extra which may or may not be added to the other activities of the Church, but is an integral part of its very being.

It was the love of God burning in him which made him see clearly that a man cannot use his energies better for the Kingdom of God than in training others in the art of Christian discipleship. The travail of bringing to the birth a new Hall in an ancient University, and of steering the vigorous infant through its early years, was no light thing. But Chavasse knew that he who builds Christian character builds for the eternal welfare of those for whom Christ died. In the latter years of his life, he looked with longing eyes to the new Universities, and prayed that there a light might shine such as he saw burning at St. Aldate's, at St. Peter's Hall, and at Wycliffe Hall, of whose Governing Body for many years he was the Chairman. One of the greatest joys of his closing years was to see well established a Theological College at Rochester, with some forty men in training for Holy Orders—this passion burned on to the end.

It was the love of God burning in him which made him the formative influence in the founding of St. Michael's House, Oxford. We think of him essentially as a man's man. But he had the vision to see—what some are so slow to glimpse to-day— that women as women have a place to fill in the ministry of the Church, a place that no man can fulfil. He did not campaign for the ordination of women. He planned for their training, in the hope that the Church would rouse itself from its lethargy and give them a place in its service proportionate to the design of God and the gifts which they are waiting to exercise.

It was the love of God burning in him which, with a charity towards others of differing views which deepened as years went by, made him long that the distinctive elements of the Evangelical tradition in the Church of England should be given their due place, should be valued, cherished, and propagated. He realized that an Anglicanism which sat loose to this part of its tradition, or which relegated it to an inferior place in its counsels, would be an Anglicanism emasculated and impoverished.

The *love of God*—yes, it was there in abundant measure. And the *steady endurance, the steadfastness, of Christ*. What other than this could have enabled him to face with such splendid courage the long years of physical disability, particularly hard for one with such an athletic record as his? What other than this could have made him so stalwart a leader during the twenty years of his episcopate at Rochester? They were years of war, when "bomb-alley" ran through his diocese up to London; and post-war years when he had to face vast problems of reconstruction and of the provision of the Church's ministry for great numbers of newcomers to the diocese. But it was all tackled with high courage, with infectious good humour, and with a steady endurance which he drew from the Lord Himself.

The love of God and the steadfastness of Christ. This was the soil out of which his own soul grew and out of which his life-work sprang. But there were other elements which contributed richly to his flowering.

Those of us who knew him well will remember how constantly he referred to his father, the saintly Bishop of Liverpool, whose Chaplain he was for some years. The eldest son drank deep of the wells from which his father drew his strength—a simple devotion to Jesus Christ, a deep Biblical piety, a happy family life.

That was the background of his youth. And, all through the rough and tumble of a very active ministry, Chavasse had behind him the stability and peace of a wonderful home and the support and sympathy of a life-companion wholly devoted to him and his work. He could not have begun to achieve what he did if it had not been for her at his side.

I ask, in conclusion, what message Christopher Chavasse would give if he could speak to us to-day in this Cathedral, which was the centre of his work for two busy decades. Or, rather, if I may put the question more accurately, I ask what in fact this man of God says to the Church to-day, for he "being dead yet speaketh".

First of all, and above all, I think he says to us: Keep the fires of your love of God burning bright. All the machinery of the Church, all the organization which we so easily proliferate, is of little use if the first love is left. And then: Watch that steadfastness, the solid, dogged perseverance which enables a disciple, having set his hand to the plough, never to look back; that endurance which makes a man walk and not faint, even if he cannot always mount up with wings as eagles, or run and not be weary.

And to what practical tasks would he bid us address ourselves? High on his list of priorities would, I doubt not, be the task of evangelism, the confrontation of men, women and children with Christ in His glory, and the challenging of them with His demand for their allegiance. Men and women in the Universities old and new; men and women in the housing estates; men and women in the great houses and the humble cottages of our land—no matter who they are or where they are, they must have the opportunity of meeting Christ!

Not far below this on his list of priorities would be the training of young men and women for lives of service. There is wastage of man-power—and even more of woman-power to-day —because there are not enough people with the vision which Chavasse had to spot them, to challenge them, to train them, and to launch them into the thick of the fight, taking risks all the time!

To this he summons us. One other message comes direct to us from that life so fully lived, though I doubt whether he often spoke of it himself. He tells us how suffering can be taken up and used creatively by the power of God. He showed us that for twenty long years. He speaks of it still.

"Continue"—he says, taking up the words of the Apostle— "continue in the things thou hast learned. Preach the Word. Be instant in season, out of season. Watch. Endure. Do the work of an evangelist. Make full proof of thy ministry. And the Lord direct your hearts towards God's love and the steadfastness of Christ!"

7

CHRISTIAN EDUCATION

Put on the whole armour of God (Ephesians 6:11)

A sermon preached to the Annual Conference of the National Union of Teachers in Scarborough Parish Church, April 22, 1962

7

THE SITUATION WHICH faces the modern educationist is not an easy one. It would probably be true to say that the schoolteacher of to-day carries a heavier weight of responsibility in relation to his pupils than did his predecessors of a generation ago, because, in so many cases, there is instability in the homes from which the children come. I do not intend to quote figures in regard to the number of divorce cases in this country per annum. You know, far better than I, the chaos created in a child's mind when he, or she, does not know which of two homes he is to go to next holidays, and the effects of this home instability on his health and general character. Nor need I elaborate the effect on many of that general feeling of uncertainty—even of fear—which is the malaise of a generation of parents who have never lived in days which were not days of war hot or cold. Small wonder, then, if the child of such parents is tempted to succumb to the old adage: "Let us eat and drink, for to-morrow we die." We sympathize with the boy who, when asked what he hoped to be when he grew up, replied with the one word, "Alive!"

Again, it is all too easy for a youngster, as he advances from junior to senior, to feel oppressed by what J. S. Mill called "the disastrous feeling of not worthwhile" when he begins to ponder world forces far beyond his control, mass movements which he can do terribly little to manipulate, energies of nature liberated by men who now find themselves unable to control them. "What am I?" he may well ask; and he may find himself tempted to reply: "A speck on a world which itself is but a speck in a universe of unimaginable proportions; a digit; a powerless nonentity." Or again, he finds himself growing up in a world in which the word *vocation* is rarely used, except in the negative sentence: "He has missed his vocation." "What are you going to *do*, or to *be*?" he is frequently asked. But he would raise his eyebrows in surprise if someone said, "What is

57

your vocation?" More's the pity, for the word vocation implies a God who *minds* what a youngster becomes, how he exercises his gifts, what he does with his life; and it implies the ability on the boy's part to obey—or for that matter to disobey—that vocation.

The atmosphere around the youngster of to-day, for all the benefits of a Welfare State, is hardly conducive to the building of strong Christian character. It was one of your own number who, in a recent edition of a great national daily, pointed out that the teacher's task is not made easier when "pornography has become the stock-in-trade of at least one mass-circulation newspaper; and governments not only legalize gambling, but have formidable stakes in the business as well; when local authorities license betting-shops next door to the very schools they are called on to maintain, and when the cinema industry and television authorities have become purveyors of violence and depravity." I myself would add: "When schoolchildren can buy contraceptives at local shops, and no questions be asked as to the age or status of the customer."

It has been said—I think with a measure of correctness—that much modern art and some Christian literature is better at reflecting society's ills than at pointing to their cure. I do not intend to fall into that error in this sermon. If I have pointed out a few of the factors which make the growth of to-day's child into a full and healthy manhood or womanhood a matter of difficulty, I have done so only to make the point that the *onus* on the schoolteacher to-day is extremely heavy.

None of us who takes our work seriously ever imagined that our task was merely the cramming of the children with facts, so that in due course they might defeat the examiners at whatever particular educational crisis lay ahead of them. We do not attempt to produce walking encyclopaedias even in abridged editions. But we do need constantly to remind ourselves of the fact that, by philological derivation and in actual hard practice, the task of education is precisely so to *nourish* and *rear* the child that he may experience fulness of life; that he may be *healthy* in character; that he may be whole.

We may say that it is not right that such a weight of responsibility should in so many cases rest on the shoulders of the schoolteacher; the heavier end should be borne by the parents. Indeed, it should. But it is part of the sickness of modern society that many parents have abdicated from their share in that responsibility, and those who teach must take on the extra load if the child is to be saved from disaster. That is to say, the school-teacher to-day finds himself necessarily concerned with the total health and with the character-formation of the child in his care. That, whether he welcomes the fact or not, is involved in the very nature of education, and its urgency is made the greater by the particular state of the society of which teacher and child are members.

If what I have said is broadly true, it is enough to make us tremble (and I venture to say "us" rather than "you", for much of my working life has been that of a teacher, though the age of my students has been higher than is that of yours). "Do you work in fear and trembling?" said Blake to Samuel Palmer, who had come to sit at his feet. "Indeed I do, sir." "Then you'll do," answered the master.

I should tremble to send any child of mine to a teacher who did not tremble before the immensity and the delicacy of his task! Spencer Leeson, that great headmaster, first of Merchant Taylors' School and then of Winchester, was, so far as technical qualifications and knowledge of affairs were concerned, better equipped than most people for the task of education. But in writing to a friend, himself about to become a headmaster, Leeson confessed that it was only when he looked down at the sea of boys' faces that he felt his utter inadequacy to discharge his responsibilities. He wrote: "My own religious faith came to me in full force as soon as I realized I was responsible for the spiritual care of many others . . . Moreover only on the footing of religious faith can anybody hope to give a purpose to educa-tion that is worth anything." I pass that on for what it is worth —the conviction of a man of great experience that *knowledge* is not enough if you are really to minister to those who will be to-morrow's men and women; and so to minister as to put them in the way of wholeness, holiness and character.

Which brings us back to our text. The enemies facing our children to-day are legion, and their weapons destructive of much that we ourselves hold to be more precious than life

59

itself. What can we do, not simply to *protect* them, but to equip them in their turn to strike a blow for righteousness and truth? I believe the only full and adequate answer is to be found in putting them in the way of understanding our text: "Put on the whole armour of God"—that they may be able to withstand in the evil day, and having done all, to stand. There is character. There is health for the whole man. There is holiness. There is, in every one who begins to grasp this, that element of stability which a rootless society so desperately needs.

You ask me what I mean when I use this picture language of the text? I can only answer in terms of the religion which has meant and still means life to me. I believe that the greatest thing that any man can do for a child is to put him on the path of Jesus Christ in such a way that the two of them can walk together throughout life. To effect such an introduction is to save a child from drifting, to give him a purpose, and to set his life within the dimensions of eternity without which his standards tend to waver and his values to slip. On that path and in that friendship, he will see, as nowhere else, that service is more important than money or fame, and that caring for the eternal welfare of others (which is what the New Testament calls *love*) is the only finally worthwhile thing in life.

I have used phrases about "putting a child on to the path of Jesus Christ" and "effecting an introduction" between our Lord and a child. This is obviously very much more than giving the child a mild dose of innocuous religion. If this is to be done —and I doubt whether less than this is worth much in view of the strength and subtlety of the enemy—our Lord Jesus Christ will have to be presented as very much more than a mere historical figure or a great ethical teacher. The child will have to see Him in some such way as the New Testament presents Him—

As Saviour to be received:
as Master to be served:
as Head of the Church to be worshipped:
as Lord of History and Light of life,
with Whom men shall not walk in darkness,
without Whom they stumble and fall.

It was Dean Inge, I believe, who first said that religion is caught rather than taught. That was a dangerous half-truth, for the steady *teaching* of the Faith as that which gives meaning to life is one of the most urgent tasks in your calling. But there was this of truth in Inge's dictum—that while anyone can teach the facts of Christianity (the story contained in the Gospels, the journeys of St. Paul, and what have you), it takes much more than this on the part of the teacher if a boy or girl is to get a living faith. The odds are that he will catch it from one who himself is gloriously infected. *Thus* he will become a committed Christian, a man who knows how to pray, how to live, and how to die. And can we conceive of our task in any narrower terms than these?

If, faced with such a task as this, we feel our own inadequacy, we may take courage from the fact that, behind the teacher humble enough to acknowledge his need, stands another Teacher. His wisdom and love are available through that Holy Spirit whose never-ceasing task it is to make Jesus our great Contemporary. As we turn to take up that task in all its great dimensions, we can hear Him say:

"Come unto Me.
Take my yoke upon you.
Learn of me."

And, in obedience to what is at once an invitation and a command, we shall find rest to our souls and life that is life indeed for those committed to our charge.

8

MAKING THE MYSTERY CLEAR

[Pray] that I may make it clear, as I ought to speak
(Colossians 4 : 4, *Revised Standard Version*)

A sermon preached before the University of Oxford, January 29, 1961

8

THE WORLD OF the first century into which Christianity was born was a world in which secret cults abounded. These cults had a language of their own—their adherents loved to talk of mysteries, and initiates, and intermediary beings between that world and this world of evil matter, of light and darkness, of *gnosis*, "knowledge". Saul of Tarsus, Jew though he was, grew up in a town where this language was part of the linguistic coinage in use every day. When, as a Christian Apostle, he later came to write his letters, he found himself using the language of the cults. Perhaps such language had become part of the jargon of the day, in much the same way as certain scientific terms have become part of our vocabulary though many of us would find it hard to define these terms in such a way as would satisfy the experts. Perhaps he used these terms the better to catch the ear of those whom he wished to reach with his message. Anyhow he used them—and *mysterion*, "mystery", is a case in point. The strange thing, however, is that he used this word not in the context of something hidden for the benefit of initiates only but of something made known for the benefit of all. "It is a particularly pointed paradox," says Professor C. F. D. Moule, "to speak of *mysterion* in connection with *phaneroun* (verse 4) when that verb means (as it does here) a public manifestation." St. Paul's use of the term may be compared to the case of a doctor who, in the course of his work, lights upon a cure for some fell disease; thereafter his only concern is to make known what has hitherto been hidden from the eyes of men.

It is precisely because St. Paul, in common with all the great writers of the New Testament, believed that the Gospel did provide and offer a cure for man's radical disease of sin and maladjustment with God and his neighbours, that his one consuming passion was to make clear that which, prior to the coming of our Lord Jesus Christ, had been hidden or at best

E

seen only in shadow. To the declaration of that mystery, to the making plain of that good news he devoted all his considerable powers, and for it he eventually died.

The health of the Church at any given time may, in large part, be judged by the care that she is giving to just this task. Is she making the mystery of Christ plain as she ought to speak? Is that the primary task to which she is bending her energies and for which she is training her best men? Or, on the other hand, is she allowing herself to be side-tracked into other tasks which, however worthy, are contributing more to her own glory than to the magnifying and clarifying of her message? These are questions of fundamental importance. The Church must never allow herself to be deflected from giving her closest attention to them.

I venture this morning to draw your attention to this question in connection with two matters which are engaging the thinking of some of the best minds in the Church to-day. I refer, first, to the revising of the Church's basic documents, and, secondly, to the staffing and succouring of the younger churches overseas. These two matters, though apparently so different the one from the other, have this in common that they both aim at making clear the mystery of Christ.

I. *The revising of the Church's basic documents*

It is a strange and undeniable fact that the cutting edge of a document gets blunted with the passing of the years. That is *partly* due to the nature of language. Words are like coins whose image and superscription wear thin the more they are rubbed and the older they get. It is *partly* due to the change in social climate which takes place as century gives way to succeeding century. It was all right in the seventeenth century for the catechist to address the catechumen as "my good child" and to exhort him to order himself "lowly and reverently to all his betters". But to-day such an approach is hardly likely to commend itself to, or win the confidence of, the catechumen! The loss of cutting edge is *partly* due to the sheer deadening effect of repetition. One can hear a powerful phrase so often that its power fails to register, as a man may hear the noise of an alarm

66

clock which, though once it woke him with a start, now leaves him slumbering soundly.

All these things demand that from time to time the Church should look again at her basic documents and ask whether they are doing what they are intended to do. If not, then some very careful thought must be given to their re-fitting for the task.

As a matter of fact, that is precisely what the Church is doing at the present moment, and doing with very considerable energy. If those who are engaged in this difficult but interesting and important task are allowed to get on with their work unimpeded by an undue conservatism or distaste for change on the part of those who from earliest days have learned to love the old forms, then I believe the Church will be provided with means by which she may do her work with considerably greater efficiency and power, the work of making plain for all to see the mystery of Christ as she ought to do.

In this connection I mention, first of all, the new English translation of the New Testament.[1] Here is no revision of a translation, such as are some of the versions of the Scriptures now in our hands. Here is the best translation which the best scholars can produce, from the best manuscripts so far as these scholars are able to assess their worth. If we may be permitted to doubt whether there is such a thing as the "timeless English" into which the scholars have tried to translate the Greek, yet they have achieved a splendid combination of liveliness and dignity. Though the book is not intended primarily for reading in Church, it would be my personal hope that the various Churches will, through their governing bodies, encourage the reading of the New Testament Lessons from this version. If we meet with resistance, then we must patiently and persistently remind our critics that the new wine of the Gospel must be put into new vessels. If the Church does not attend to this, the Scriptures, mighty as they are, will become, as did the prophetic word to Ezekiel's hearers, like "a very lovely song of one that hath a pleasant voice and can play well on an instrument" —and that will be all. From that peril may our Church and people be delivered.

I turn next to the revised form of the Catechism of the Church

[1] *The New English Bible: New Testament* was published on March 14, 1961.

of England which has been presented to the Convocations and received general approval. This does not mean that it at once becomes the official Catechism of the Church of England. It will come before the Convocations again and will no doubt undergo certain alterations before reaching its final form.[1] This Revised Catechism is the result of some hard work on the part of a Commission set up by the Archbishops of Canterbury and York. Not only have the members of the Commission modernized the language with a far greater measure of freedom than they would have done had they been revising a *service* of the Church, they have also extended the scope and range of the teaching contained in the Catechism, adding a great deal of material, for example, on the Church, the means of grace, the Bible, Christian duty, and the Christian hope. In so doing its authors have taken note of the results of the revival of Biblical scholarship. In the eschatological section entitled "The Christian Hope", they have recognized the importance of making clear at least an outline of that Christian doctrine which occupies so large a place in the Biblical revelation. The importance of stressing this particular aspect of Christian doctrine is the greater because Communism has a hope of its own, clearly defined and enunciated, albeit confined to this world alone.

It is to be hoped that the Church will not be side-tracked in any way in its consideration of this document by allowing proctors in Convocation or members of the Press to fasten on such minor matters as the omission of specific reference to the devil! His satanic Majesty no doubt realizes that we are seeking to put into the hands of the Church's teachers a document which I doubt not will help them in no small way to make clear the mystery of Christ. To side-track us in this work might well be one of his more wily devices!

Thirdly, I would mention the Revised Psalter. Two years ago a small Commission was appointed to "produce for consideration by the Convocations a revision of the text of the Psalter designed to remove obscurities and serious errors of translation, yet such as to retain as far as possible the general character and

---

[1] *The Revised Catechism* for the Church of England was published on February 27, 1962, "commended for use in teaching for a period of seven years by the Convocations of Canterbury and York at the sessions of January, 1962."

style and rhythm of Coverdale's version and its suitability for congregational use". This Commission has been steadily at work, and very shortly will produce for consideration of the Convocations its revision of the 1st Book of Psalms, 1–41, together with a Preface explaining the principles under which the members have worked. If general approval is given to this conservative revision, work will proceed.[1] It will then be possible to put into the hands of Churchmen a version of the Psalms which in parts will differ little (or even not at all) from the familiar version of Coverdale, but in other parts will convey much more clearly the sense of the original and will avoid some words which to modern ears have become almost meaningless.

Further, though it has not been the task of the Commission to point the Psalms, great care is being given to their "pointability", so that it is not beyond the bounds of hope that gradually there will spread throughout the Church of England a uniform system of pointing—an end greatly to be desired. We have not been asked to produce what we consider to be the choicest parts of the Psalter to be used in the worship of the Church. We have been asked to produce *all* the Psalms, and it will, I hope, be for others in due course to cull from this work the best for public worship. If the Psalms, which were the hymn book of the Jewish Church, were part of the preparation for the coming of Christ (and few would dispute this), then we may maintain that their revision has its place, even if only a small place, in that making clear the mystery of Christ of which we are here and now thinking.

I come now to the second of my main points.

II. *The staffing and succouring of the younger churches overseas*

The last century and a half has seen a phenomenal extension of the Church throughout the world. Professor Latourette has said that it seems incontestable that the great advance of Christianity between 1815 and 1914 left a greater impress upon mankind than did any previous advance. We have exported

[1] Approval was given, and work has proceeded and is proceeding. It is hoped that the revision of the whole Psalter will be completed in 1963.

some of our best men and women who have given lavishly of themselves and of their skills—in the ministry of Word and Sacrament, in medicine, in education, in a thousand different ways. That giving is still going on. But it is a fact which the authorities in the Missionary Societies corroborate only too readily, that the progress of the missionary task is hindered to-day mainly by two causes.

The first is the lack of money. That is serious enough. One set of figures will suffice to illustrate this. In 1920 in the dioceses of the Provinces of Canterbury and York, of every £100 of expenditure, £8 12s. went on overseas missions. In 1956 that figure had dropped to £3 2s. The second cause is the lack of manpower, and this is no less serious than is the lack of money. In nothing like sufficient numbers are young men and women offering themselves for the service of Christ abroad wherever He wants them. What are the reasons for this? No doubt there are many. For example, there is a false idea abroad that the East no longer needs or welcomes the help of the West. This is a very dangerous half-truth. The fact is that the younger churches still greatly need the skills that we can supply, indeed they welcome them, provided that such skills are given in the spirit of the helper who is willing to stand behind the local leader, largely hidden, and in the capacity of one who is willing to be among them as one that serveth.

Another reason may be that the idea of security is so much "in the air" to-day that almost without our realizing it such a consideration is allowed to affect our thinking and planning. The Welfare State which cares for a man from womb to tomb has provided an atmosphere in which it is not easy—I do not say it is impossible—for a man or woman to think of the throwing away of life (as it would seem to many), of the abandonment of opportunities for advancement, of the losing of life if so be that others may by that loss find Christ and be found in Him.

But perhaps deeper and more profound than either of these reasons for the lack of an adequate supply of helpers for the churches overseas is this—all too easily we fail to grasp the concept of the mystery of Christ as being the supreme treasure, the pearl of great price, which has been entrusted to us to make plain to others. We regard it as something to be discussed, to be

70

argued about, to be tossed to and fro in the rough and tumble of debate. But "a secret to be made plain"—? A thing given by God to be received and passed on, or, better, a Person revealed to be known, loved and shared—that perhaps is a notion hardly congenial to a generation which finds it easier to discuss rather than to decide, to debate rather than to plunge. Let it not be thought that I see no place for the thrust and parry of debate. Indeed I do. I am only making the point that such debate must lead to action, to the place where a man says: "Here I stand: I can no other", to the place of committal for Christ's sake and for the sake of the world for which He was contented to be betrayed.

If the Cross on which Jesus died be the great divide of history; if the redemption which is in Christ Jesus our Lord be the unique thing which the Scriptures declare it to be and which millions find it to be; if Christ be indeed the very Son of God who for us men and for our salvation came down from heaven, died, rose and lives victorious; if this be true, then I take sides, I act, I commit, I abandon, I serve, I give my life to make clear the mystery of Christ.

I give my life—yes. But I *live* my life, in such a way as to make plain the mystery of Christ. For, when all is said and done, it is the life lived to God's glory and in dedication to His service which more than anything else serves to make plain the mystery of Christ. There are millions who will never read the New English Bible, or the Revised Catechism, or the Revised Psalter. They may not read any of the Four Gospels, but they are bound to read the *fifth* gospel, the gospel according to *you*, when they are confronted by you in the rough and tumble of the playing-field, or the lab, or the lecture room, or the coffee party. There you, if you are a committed Christian, make the mystery of Christ plain, in some such way as the Son of God manifested the glory of the Father in His Incarnate Person, at carpenter's bench or in humble cottage home. The Word became flesh and we beheld His glory—He declared the Father.

I cannot close this University sermon to-day without reminding you that St. Paul sets this theme of making plain the mystery of Christ in the context of prayer. "Praying also for us that . . ." If the Church is not a body which gives absolute priority to prayer, it becomes like a machine running without oil. It will only grind its way with noisy cacophony, a menace to itself and a danger to everyone concerned. But if it be indeed the Body of Christ, holding up holy hands in intercession and blessing, then there is no limit to what we in our own generation may see of the spread of the faith, of the coming of the light, of the making plain the mystery of Christ. And for those of us who in the Church are called to positions of grave responsibility, I would ask, more than for anything else, the sustaining prayers of the faithful. Advice we shall have—and welcome it. Criticism we shall have in plenty—and I doubt not benefit from it. But the one thing we cannot do without is the prayer, sustained and sustaining, of the faithful: that, whatever else we do or leave undone, we may make clear the mystery of Christ.

9

HOW JESUS RAN HIS LIFE

An Exposition of St. Mark 1 : 35–45, printed in *Lenten Counsellors, A Catena of Lent Sermons* (A. R. Mowbray and Co. Ltd., 1962)

9

IF YOU WANT to see how Jesus ran His life, you will find it summed up admirably in the last eleven verses of the first chapter of St. Mark. It would be worth your while to read these verses over slowly and carefully in any version of the New Testament which you have by you, and then to say to yourself: "This is how He ran His life. Is it a pointer as to how I should run mine?" What better theme for Lenten meditation and resolve could there be than that?

And in the morning, rising up a great while before day, He went out, and departed into a solitary place, and there prayed.

And Simon and they that were with Him followed after Him. And when they had found Him, they said unto Him, All men seek for Thee.

And He said unto them, Let us go into the next towns, that I may preach there also: for therefore came I forth.

And He preached in their synagogues throughout all Galilee, and cast out devils.

And there came a leper to Him, beseeching Him, and kneeling down to Him, and saying unto Him, If thou wilt, thou canst make me clean.

And Jesus, moved with compassion, put forth His hand, and touched him, and saith unto him, I will: be thou clean.

And as soon as He had spoken, immediately the leprosy departed from him, and he was cleansed.

And He straitly charged him, and forthwith sent him away; and saith unto him, See thou say nothing to any man: but go thy way, shew thyself to the priest, and offer for thy cleansing those things which Moses commanded, for a testimony unto them.

But he went out, and began to publish it much, and to blaze abroad the matter, insomuch that Jesus could no more openly enter into the city, but was without in desert places: and they came to Him from every quarter (*St. Mark* 1 : 35–45).

There, with three broad strokes of his pen, St. Mark delineates the pattern of the life and ministry of Jesus. We could summarize it like this—withdrawal; proclamation; compassion. Let us look at each in turn.

I. *Withdrawal*

First-century Palestine was no place of idyllic calm. True, Galilee in springtime was—and is—a lovely place, with its luxuriant growth of wild flowers and its shimmering lake. But Jesus came to a land where there was no Welfare State, no Health Service of any kind, no pensions; a land occupied by an enemy invader; a land where taxation was very high and fear was on every side. He came to His public ministry conscious of mighty powers latent within Him; conscious, too, of a vast work waiting to be done among a desperately needy people. He came as a great worker—"My Father worketh hitherto," He said, "and I work." He came as a fighter—never resigned to or acquiescent in the ills which He saw around Him, but prepared to go into battle against the evils of sin, ignorance and disease.

Yet this Jesus, conscious of His powers as healer, preacher and teacher, and with the evidence of His powers all around Him in the healed souls and bodies of His friends, this Jesus used to drop everything and *withdraw*. "And in the morning, rising up a great while before day, He went out, and departed into a solitary place, and there prayed." He withdrew *early*, before the sun was up and the pressure of the day's events was on Him. He withdrew to a *lonely* place, partly because He was vividly conscious of God in nature, and partly, perhaps, because He lived in a crowded home and must needs be alone with God. "What a waste of time," we say. He knew better than that. He knew that power drained out of Him as He gave Himself to needy people (St. Mark 5 : 30). So it was that He established a rhythm, a pattern, for His living—withdrawal before work; retreat before attack; renewal before advance.

Nature taught Him the beneficence of that pattern—the recess of the tides before their advance; the sleep of the night before the activity of the day; the inertia of the winter and the opening of the hungry mouth of the fields before the quick and lush growth of spring and summer. And *Scripture* taught Him the blessing of Sabbath rest before six days of toil. He learnt the lesson well.

II. *Proclamation*

"And He said unto them, Let us go into the next towns, that I may preach there also; for therefore came I forth. And He preached in their synagogues throughout all Galilee, and cast out devils." John Baptist's preaching ministry had been silenced by his arrest and imprisonment (1 : 14), but the work must go on. Within our Lord there burned a great passion to proclaim the divine word, the only message which would meet the deep need of His hearers. So He heralded the good news of God as Father—love at the heart of the universe; and God as King—law and order at the heart of the universe. Love and law, calling for the answer of love and obedience from God's people. There was a Kingdom to be entered, and its entrance might be missed. There was a heaven to be gained and a hell to be avoided. This was a Man with a message of momentous importance.

And—this to be noted, for it is in marked contrast to the prophets of the Old Testament and the saints of the Christian era—the Man was Himself central to His message. "Come unto *Me*," He cried to the weary and heavy-laden, "and *I* will give you rest. Take *My* yoke . . . learn of *Me* . . ." In Him the Kingdom of Heaven had arrived. In Him man faced something greater than law or temple.

III. *Compassion*

The scene recorded in verses 40–45 is one of consummate courage, physical and moral. To touch a leper was not only to incur physical danger, but to defile oneself in the eyes of those who observed the law. But when Jesus was faced with deep human need, caution went to the winds and compassion took over—"He stretched out His hand and touched him"! *People* mattered more than regulations, the mending of broken men and women. To that He dedicated Himself, till they said of Him, "Himself took our infirmities and bare our sicknesses" (St. Matt. 8:17). He never quenched the smoking flax, He fanned it to a flame.

Confronted by this leper, there was that within our Lord for which there was no expression in mere words. "He *touched* him." There are things which the lips cannot say but the hands can. "The highest cannot be spoken, it can only be acted," said

Goethe. Hence the whole sacramental principle. Hence the Word becoming flesh, the Incarnation which is the acting out of God's love and grace on the scene of history.

When Ananias, unwilling and fearful, was sent to Saul, who till so recently had been the arch-persecutor of the Christian disciples, before he spoke to him he *put his hands on him.* Only then did he say—and what graciousness there was in the title!—*"Brother* Saul." His compassion, like the compassion of the Lord, came through his fingers as well as through his lips (Acts 9: 17).

Here, then, was the pattern of the life and ministry of Jesus—withdrawal, proclamation, compassion. This was

the way the Master went;
Should not the servant tread it still?

I. *Withdrawal*

"Withdrawal? Impossible! We are far too busy! Leave that to the mystics and the contemplatives. It is not for the ordinary Christian." Are you sure? Or is that the voice of "our Father Below", as C. S. Lewis called the devil, who knows that if he can ruin that, all is ruined? The principle is easy to see. It is hard to learn and obey. But the virility of our spiritual life hangs on its observance.

The student and the business man or woman can learn this by the use of an alarm clock and the expedient of not going to bed too late! For the mother of a young family where there is little or no help in the home, the problem is much more difficult. But even there, where the early morning demands on her are too clamant to allow of quiet then, she can generally carve out a few minutes, perhaps in the middle of the day or after the children are in bed, for that withdrawal with her Lord, without which life can become barren and tempers frayed.

"But what do we *do* in those times of withdrawal?" That is for you to find out and to work out. Apart from the work of intercession, ordered and planned, I would mention two things: first, what I would call *exploration.* God is so great, and we little creatures only know the outskirts of His ways. The God of some of us is so small that he is not much bigger than ourselves! But the divine Name (Exod. 3: 14) probably means, "I will become what I will become." This is the God who increasingly reveals Himself to the reverent explorer. Wonder is akin to worship, and indeed is part of it. "My God, how wonderful Thou art . . .!"

Secondly, *learning to be quiet*. We shall never stretch out a firm hand to those who are being battered by the storms of life until we ourselves have learnt to be quiet in the presence of Jesus. The emphasis of the Prayer Book collects on "passing our time in rest and quietness", or "pardon and peace, that they may . . . serve . . . with a quiet mind" is not a selfish emphasis. It is simply echoing the New Testament injunction to come to Jesus, to learn of Him, to take His yoke, and so find rest to our souls. That is the only way to a heart at leisure from itself. And only a person with such a heart can minister to others.

We must pray the old prayer with realism and determination :

> Lord, temper with tranquillity
> Our manifold activity,
> That we may do our work for Thee
> With very great simplicity.

So we learn in periods of withdrawal, to press our weakness close to the divine strength ; our sin close to divine forgiveness ; our ignorance close to divine wisdom ; our lovelessness close to divine love ; our self-pity close to divine self-giving. We begin to find the secret which Mrs. Browning expressed in the lines :

> I smiled to think God's greatness
> Flowed around our incompleteness,
> Round our restlessness
> His rest.

II. *Proclamation*

"I'm no preacher, and never shall be. I could not preach to save my life." That may be. But whether you like it or not, you are a herald, a proclaimer of your Lord. All Christian living is proclamatory. By life as well as by lip, if you are a Christian in touch with your Master, you preach not yourself, but Christ Jesus as Lord, and yourself as the servant of His followers, for His sake. You are the bearer of a message which is the answer to *worry*. I do not find that worry has gone from the average man's life because the Welfare State has made his material existence easier. It is not so easy as that. A man needs to know God as Father before he can find the answer to worry and to fear. You are the bearer of a message which is the answer to *sin*, that radical self-centredness which is the curse of us all, that idolatry which enthrones self and dethrones God from His rightful place, which stultifies communion with God, and spoils our relationships with others.

III. *Compassion*

It is only another name for love. And love is caring, caring with the deep care of God.

Love has been defined by Bishop Stephen Neill as "the set of the will for the eternal welfare of another". Note the stress on will. Love is an affair, not primarily of the emotions but of the will, so that we can *love* someone whom we do not naturally like. And it is directed to the other person's *eternal* welfare. So it may well correspond with the description of a Northern saint which ran like this: "He was strangely austere, strangely tender; strangely gentle, strangely inflexible."

For this compassionate living, thank God, there are divine resources available. "The love of God is shed abroad in our hearts by the Holy Spirit given to us." The phrase "shed abroad" is the same as that used in Joel—of the pouring out of the Holy Spirit on God's servants. Thus God's compassion comes through the Christian to meet and to succour those who are in need, in loneliness, in distress. Thus gradually and bit by bit the marks of St. Paul's great hymn to love, given us in 1 Corinthians 13, are seen in us, and we become a blessing to others.

Withdrawal, proclamation, compassion—this was the pattern of the life of Jesus. In so far as the Church which is His Body follows that pattern, so far will it continue His work in the world. But let us not be vague and general. That means *you*, doesn't it? And it means *me*.

IO

NEW DELHI AND YOU

The Word was made flesh, and dwelt among us, and we beheld His glory . . . (St. John 1 : 14)

A sermon preached in Beverley Minster, Yorkshire, December 24, 1961

F

10

THREE WEEKS AGO I was in Delhi. It was my first visit
to India. There is always a temptation to a traveller to
write a book or speak with naïve "authority" about a
place which he has visited all too briefly. I hope I shall not fall
into such a trap. But, naturally enough, my mind is full of that
colourful sub-continent, and particularly of the tiny bit of it in
which I lived and worked for nearly three weeks. So let me start
from India. It will make a good jumping-off ground for what I
want to say to you this Christmas Eve.

Apart from the beauty which I saw all around me—beauty
of sunshine and deep blue sky, beauty of flower and bird, of
vivid colour and of local art and architecture—I think the over-
whelming impression I have brought home with me is the
impression of a land of contrasts. India is a land whose culture
goes back thousands of years; and yet its rate of illiteracy is
appallingly high. India is a land whose technical skills are considerable, and whose wealth is, in places, great—witness the
beautiful houses of New Delhi; and yet the poverty of great
masses of the people is such as to impress a traveller from our
Welfare State country with mental pictures which are indelible
for their pathos. And so one could go on. But I did not go to
India to sightsee, though I fitted a bit of that into my programme. I went as one of the delegates to the Assembly of the
World Council of Churches.

It was a remarkable gathering in many ways. Numerically
and from the point of view of organization, it was a considerable
achievement. There were some 625 official delegates there; but,
by the time you have added observers and translators and so on,
the number would be nearly doubled. There was such a variety
of tongues spoken that the speeches had to be translated from
English into German, French and Russian, and, even then,
there were many who laboured under real difficulties. The
variety of dress worn reflected the variety of nationalities and of

83

Church allegiance represented. The closing service was conducted by an Indian Church leader, and the address given by a German, Martin Niemöller. (We sent a message of loving greetings to the East German delegates and others who had been refused permission to leave their country.) It was a gathering remarkable for its variety.

But it was even more remarkable for its unity. There was much that made it difficult for us to understand one another. I am not referring to differences of language only. I am thinking of long years—often centuries—when we could only have the most slender contact with one another, years when different traditions have grown up and, naturally enough, misunderstandings have deepened. All that and a great deal besides—one might mention political differences between East and West—made for differences of viewpoint and conviction. But, above all that and over-riding all that, there was a unity which was most impressive. *We were one in Christ.* We were all deeply indebted to Him who, through various ways and forms, had become our Saviour and Lord. To me, one of the great moments of the Assembly was when a packed congregation in the Cathedral at New Delhi, representing many nations, sang together the lines:

> Jesus out of every nation
> Hath redeemed us by His blood.

In the words so often used during the Assembly, Jesus had become to us the *Light* of the World. That does not mean that we saw an easy answer to all our problems, individual or on a world scale. Far from it. We spent much of our time in the Assembly wrestling with problems created by man's sin and rebellion against God—problems of war and hunger and illiteracy and homelessness. *But* it does mean that, since Christ has made Himself known to us, a light has shone on our way which makes life without Him seem like deep darkness.

And that, thank God, is the message of Christmas. "The Light" came that first Christmas day, came to His own world, even though His own folk refused to receive Him. "The Word was made flesh and dwelt among us." The loving care of God for His children, His longing for their fulness of life, took human form. There we see it in the Babe of Bethlehem—the weakness of God stronger than men! You might have thought that St. John, when he wrote these words about the Word becoming flesh, would have said, "We beheld His humiliation." There is nothing more impotent than a new-born baby, and nothing less pretentious than a baby born amidst the stench of a stable. "We beheld His weakness, His humiliation." But, no. St. John says, "We beheld His glory." For "glory" in the Bible means the *real nature* of a person, what he is really like. It is specially used in relation to God. It is what the hymn-writer meant when he wrote:

> God's Presence and His very self
> And essence all divine.

That is what we see in Jesus. We see that God is not unmoved by the kind of thing I have mentioned in regard to India—the poverty and the homelessness and the illiteracy, and the lack of hospitalization. God is not unmoved by the kind of thing that ruins *our* lives here in England and makes them dark—greed, and pride, and selfishness and lust. He sent His Son to be the Light to lighten our darkness. And that Son of God was willing to bear our griefs and carry our sorrows—all the way from Bethlehem even to the Cross.

It was this conviction, this experience, which united us at New Delhi. It was this which made us determined to show to the world, in so far as we can, the unity which is ours in Christ. It was this which compelled us to grapple with the vast problems of grief which afflict great numbers of our fellow-men; for a faith in Christ, the Word of God, which does not issue in a great compelling compassion just isn't the real thing!

Let me tell you a little more about our meetings at New Delhi. Every morning, before the ordinary work of sessions and councils and committees took place, we met together for worship and Bible study. The forms of worship varied greatly; but, whatever the form, we met together to acknowledge our dependence on God and our thankfulness to Him who had become our Light. The Bible Study sessions were interesting. The concourse was so great that we split up into three groups.

The group to which I was assigned was conducted by a young man, an Indian, from the Syrian Orthodox Church. I have a vivid mental picture of his kindly dark face, his black beard and shining white teeth; but even more of his scholarship and penetrating insight into the meaning and relevance to modern life of the passages from the Bible which we studied together. He would open up the verses of Scripture before us. We would then keep silence for a space. Open discussion would follow, anyone making what contribution he saw fit. *Or* we would quietly discuss the passage with the person sitting next to us. Then a brief summary by the leader, and we went to the day's work—to problems connected with our own disunity; to the question of how the Church can most effectively let the light of Christ shine in a dark world; to problems of witness and service in a world which is still dark, and perplexed, and afraid, and tense with suspicion and hate.

I mention this pattern of our work at New Delhi because it is, I believe, a pattern of great importance. I do not think much would have emerged from New Delhi if we had not set aside time for common worship, corporate quiet waiting upon God, and carefully planned Bible Study together. I think more of real value would have emerged if we had put greater emphasis on this, and devoted even more time and care to it. But I am quite sure that here we have got the pattern for *all* of us—not just for the leaders and delegates who went to New Delhi, but for *all* of us who want the Light to shine through us out on to a dark world.

It is certainly the way that Jesus lived His life; first, withdrawal with His Father in worship and prayer and meditation (it is clear that He knew His scriptures very thoroughly, and knew how to use them in everyday living); and then, His ministry, His service, His compassion for all in need. It is certainly the way that Jesus taught His immediate disciples to live. First, they went apart with Him, and then He sent them out to preach, teach and heal—in short, to wrestle with the wrongs that plagued their fellow-men. And it is certainly the way God intends His people to live to-day; first, the withdrawal of worship, prayer, Bible Study, both in the "aloneness" of private prayer and in the "together-ness" of common prayer and sharing in study. *Then* we are ready to go to tackle, in His strength, the needs of a dark world which calls for His light; the needs of a diseased and distressed world which calls for His compassion.

I hope I may have conveyed to you something, however little, of the spirit of the Third Assembly of the World Council of Churches at New Delhi. What matters, of course, is that you should not say: "How interesting! I'm glad to know what they did out there." But that you should say: "Now—how can we bring that to the heart of the town or village or community where we live?" What matters is that all over the country—all over the world—groups of people from different religious traditions should get together for common prayer, and for corporate study of the Bible; and that then they should say: "Christ is the Light of the World. In the Word made flesh we have seen the glory, the real nature of God. Christ has said that *we* are the light of the world. What can we do *together* about the darkness? Let us look at our own community and see the black spots there—pray, plan, and ACT. Then let us avoid a narrow parochial outlook like the plague, and take a steady look at the dark places of the world. Perhaps we shall not be able to do a great deal. We Christians in Puddlethorpe won't be able to solve the refugee problem in Jordan, or the illiteracy in India, or the poverty in South Africa. But we might, together, make a dent in it. If we hide the light, we shall lose the light. If we let the light shine, we shall increase it."

That, I believe, is the way of New Delhi. The theme of the Assembly, "Christ the Light of the World", was sub-divided into three: Unity, Witness, and Service. These three words may well be pointers as to how we can work out locally what was outlined at the Assembly.

Unity. Here in England we have still got a great deal to learn about working *together* in Christian activity—*together* facing the social problems of our community; *together* planning for the welfare of the old or of the Teddy boys; *together* studying the Bible to see what it has to say that is relevant to our modern situation; *together* planning to do our bit to relieve the refugee or provide literature for the newly literate in Africa or Asia. "Unity is strength." Too much energy—yes, let's face it, too much *money*—is being wasted in Christian strategy (or through lack of Christian strategy) by a disunity which is totally unnecessary. In many places we have made a good start in working and praying together. But we have still a long way to go.

Witness. Christian witness is telling hungry men where they can find bread. It is pointing hungry men to the Bread of Life, who is Christ. It is pointing men in the dark to Christ who is the Light of the World. It is doing what Andrew did for his own brother Peter—saying to him "We have found the Christ." It is doing what Philip did when Nathanael asked sceptically whether any good thing could come out of Nazareth. Philip said: "Come and see!" It was a very simple, direct, straightforward answer. It was good witness. "Come and see for yourself"—and so he confronted the sceptic with Jesus—and that was enough!

Service. I was in the section at the Assembly which considered the subject of Service. Again and again we found ourselves confronted by the fact that Jesus did not pursue the way of power—indeed, He constantly refused it—but He went the way of the humble Servant of God. As preacher, as teacher, as leader, He *ministered* to the crying needs of those around Him. And at the end, He took a towel, and girded Himself, and washed the disciples' feet, and so He went His way to the Cross. From Bethlehem, where the Word was made flesh, to Calvary, where the Servant-Son was crucified, it was the way of Service.

This is the message of New Delhi as it comes to us in England this Christmas Eve. But—far more important—it is, I believe, the message of *Christ* to us—the Christ of Bethlehem and the Christ of Calvary.

> It is the way the Master went;
> Should not the servant tread it still?

II

THE FUNCTION OF THE CHURCH

Hold the Lord Christ in reverence in your hearts. Be always ready with your defence whenever you are called to account for the hope that is in you, but make that defence with modesty and respect (1 St. Peter 3 : 15, *New English Bible*)

A sermon preached in Holy Trinity Church, Hull, Yorkshire, December 31, 1961

II

I AM HAPPY TO be with you at the closing service of your Tercentenary Year. This service affords us an opportunity to seek an answer to this question: Why does this church stand here, in the middle of this great city? What is its function in the community? Is it, beautiful and glorious as it is, simply an architectural monument? Is it a place mainly useful for marrying and burying? *Why is it here?*

A full answer to those questions would take a long time. But I suggest three reasons for the presence of a church in any community.

I. *It stands for worship*

I make bold to state, categorically, that the man who does not carve out a regular place in his life for the worship of Almighty God is not living as God intends him to live. Ideally, *all* our life should be worship, an offering of our work, our leisure, our love, our talents to God. So we prepare for that life of eternity when the ideal shall be fulfilled, and "His servants shall worship Him; they shall see Him face to face . . ." (Revelation 22 : 3, 4). But that ideal will not even be approximated in this life unless, systematically and thoughtfully, regular periods are carved out of our busy lives for the one purpose of worship. For when I worship, I stand, recollected, in the presence of the all-holy, the all-loving, the all-powerful, the Father who created me, the Son who redeemed me, and the Holy Spirit who sanctifies me. I do not worship in order to get something out of God. I worship Him that He may have a chance to do with me what He wills. I look at Him, and He looks at me.

Nearly six years in Yorkshire, travelling up and down its lovely dales and wolds, have taught me much about sheep, about shepherds and about sheep-dogs. How almost unbelievably intelligent those dogs are! How responsive to the slightest whistle of the shepherd! How gentle in their contacts with the sheep! What is it that makes them like that? I do not know. But I note that they spend a great deal of time sitting at the shepherd's feet, and looking up into his face. Need I apply the picture?

I come back to my text: ". . . hold the Lord Christ in reverence in your hearts. Be always ready with your defence whenever you are called to account for the hope that is in you, but make that defence with modesty and respect."

Such a relationship to Christ and such an attitude to men begins with an act of committal to our Lord, which in turn leads on to an attitude of daily discipleship. All this is fed and stimulated by worship.

II. *It stands for study*

I am not speaking to-night especially to the learned or the scholars. I am speaking to you all. In England now there are many Christians who are tongue-tied simply because they do not know the Faith. They are not ready to give an answer, "to account for the hope that is in them"; nor will they be, until they have a firmer, surer foundation of knowledge.

Now knowledge is, broadly speaking, of two kinds. First, there is knowledge of the *facts*. It is here that so many of us are deficient. What is the Faith? Why do we believe that Jesus lived, died, rose again? Why do we believe in an after-life? Why are we Anglicans? We have nothing to fear in examining the foundations of our belief. But we shall never be able to give a reason if we do not take the trouble to learn the facts.

Secondly, there is knowledge of a *person*. It is possible to take a degree in Christian theology without being a Christian, to know the facts without knowing the Person of Christ, just as it is possible to know much about the Queen without ever having met her. Christianity basically is a friendship with the Lord Christ.

Both kinds of knowledge are called for, if we are to be equipped to obey the injunction of the text. And that calls for the devotion of time, prayer, and thought to study, and particularly to study of the Bible. This is part of the cost of our discipleship. "Be ready with your defence . . ."

III. *It stands for evangelism*

We are surrounded on all sides by puzzled people, people who are perplexed by the problems of pain and of death and of fear. But, all too often, they are too dazed to come to us to "ask a reason". We must go to them.

For this the Church of God exists—to show forth the life and love of God, and to bring men and women within its radiance. God has rescued us in order that we may rescue them. We, like John the Baptist, are to be finger-posts pointing men to "the Lamb of God who takes away the sin of the world".

Worship: study: evangelism. There are other reasons for the existence of the Church of Holy Trinity in Hull, but these come pretty near the top in priority.

"Hold the Lord Christ in reverence in your hearts. Be always ready with your defence whenever you are called to account for the hope that is in you, but make that defence with modesty and respect."

Let this be your motto as you go into the new year, and into this fourth century of your church's life.

12

MINISTERS AND STEWARDS

Let a man so account of us, as of the ministers of Christ, and stewards of the mysteries of God (1 Corinthians 4:1)

An Ordination Charge, given in Bishopthorpe Chapel, York, December 16, 1961

12

THE COLLECT, EPISTLE and Gospel of the third Sunday in Advent are all admirably suited for the season when the Church turns its attention to the ordaining of deacons and priests to its ministry. The Collect and Epistle have in common a reference to "ministers and stewards of the mysteries of God", while the Gospel is devoted to a story about John the Baptist, who gave his life in fulfilment of his task as a faithful minister and steward of his Master.

I base my charge to you, on the eve of your Ordination, on these two words: "ministers" and "stewards". In the course of the ordination service you will be called by many titles—"watchmen", "messengers", and so on. I fasten on these two words, "ministers" and "stewards", and bid you look at them briefly.

I. *Minister* (*hypēretēs*). It is a very general word. It means one who serves a master or superior. It can be used of a doctor's assistant, of an adjutant, of a synagogue attendant. A minister is one whose task is not to draw attention to himself, but to facilitate the work of his master. Indeed, it is up to him to get out of the way, that his master may be seen.

Those of you who to-morrow are to be ordained priest will not lose the character of deacon or minister. An archbishop is still a deacon (as he is still a priest). He retains that function to the end, and the fact that he comes last in an ecclesiastical procession is a constant reminder to him of the fact that he is servant of all—he is still a *minister*.

Your function, then, is never to magnify yourself, but always to seek to magnify your Master and your office.

II. *Steward*. This is a man in charge of a treasure. He looks after his master's property. He did not create it, nor did he earn it, nor does he own it. But he is responsible to look after it.

What better word could be found by which to describe you and your trust? You are, as St. Paul said, "put in trust with the Gospel" (i Thessalonians 2: 4).

97   G

The Pastoral Epistles use a word (*parathēkē*) which means a deposit, a treasure committed to someone's trust. One of the most interesting occurrences of that word is in 2 Timothy 1:12, where the writer says, "I know whom I have believed, and am persuaded that He is able to keep that which I have committed unto Him against that day." But the phrase can equally well mean "that which He has committed unto me". This, if it be the true rendering, is of infinite comfort to those who tremble (as all of us should) at the trust which at Ordination is committed to us. In a real sense, we may think of ourselves as co-trustees with Him who puts us in trust with the Gospel.

Ours is a calling full of perils. Some men handle only a fraction of the treasure committed to them, with the result that their congregations are poor and anaemic. Others get stale in the handling of the treasure, with the result that their people miss the glory of the "many-splendoured thing". Others, again, preach themselves instead of Christ, and so men do not glimpse the treasure at all.

J. H. Moulton was a great New Testament scholar. I have no doubt that, when he wrote the poem which I am about to quote, he had in mind the class-room in which he was wont to expound the Greek Testament. For us, however, the poem is patient of a wider interpretation, and the "door" may refer to the door of your pulpit or to the door of opportunity which your ordination will open up to you:

> Lord, at thy word opens yon door, inviting
> Teacher and taught to feast this hour with thee:
> Opens a book where God in human writing
> Thinks his deep thoughts, and dead tongues live for me.
>
> Too dread the task, too great the duty calling,
> Too heavy far the weight is laid on me!
> Oh, if mine own thought should on thy words falling
> Mar the great message, and men hear not thee!
>
> Give me thy voice to speak, thine ear to listen,
> Give me thy mind to grasp the mystery;
> So shall my heart throb and my glad eyes glisten,
> Rapt with the wonders thou dost show to me.

Bishop Charles Gore, in one of his Ordination charges, spoke thus to the candidates: "To-morrow I shall say to you 'Wilt thou?', 'Wilt thou?', 'Wilt thou?' Before long, your ministry will be at an end, and Another will address these questions to you—'Hast thou?', 'Hast thou?', 'Hast thou?' "

Those are solemn words. What do they call for? Not for panic, but for quiet committal, total, sincere committal of ourselves to our Lord. "Lord, make me a minister, hidden, that Thou mayest be seen. Lord, make me a steward, faithful to my trust."

We shall use as our prayer the words of Archbishop Cosmo Gordon Lang, found after his death among his papers. They were jotted down on the eve of his Ordination as deacon on Trinity Sunday, 1890:

> O Love, I give myself to Thee,
> Thine ever, only Thine to be.

This day I consecrate all that I have or hope to be to Thy service—all that I have been I lay at the foot of Thy Cross. O Crucified Lord! forgive the sins of my past life; fold me within the embrace of Thy all-prevailing sacrifice; purify me by Thy Passion; raise me by Thy perfect submission. Son of Man, hallow all my emotions and affections; gather them to Thyself and make them strong only for Thy service, enduring through Thy Presence. Eternal Word, sanctify my thoughts; make them free with the freedom of Thy Spirit. Son of God, consecrate my will to Thyself; unite it with Thine; and so fill me with Thine own abundant life. King of Glory, my Lord and Master, take my whole being, redeem it by Thy Blood; engird it with Thy power; use it in Thy service; and draw it ever closer to Thyself. From this day forth, O Master, take my life and let it be ever, only, all for Thee.

13

THE WHOLENESS OF MAN

The Medical Inaugural Lecture, delivered at Leeds University, October 20, 1958

13

I CAN BEGIN IN no better way than by quoting a sentence from Jung. "More and more," he wrote in 1933, "we turn our attention from the visible disease and direct it upon the man as a whole" (C. G. Jung: *Modern Man in Search of a Soul*, p. 222).

"Man as a whole"—"The wholeness of man"—that is my subject to-day, a subject approached by the lecturer with some trepidation, for who am I to address a distinguished gathering of doctors and scientists and a soon-to-be-distinguished gathering of medical undergraduates?

All my working life has been spent in non-scientific circles, if, following the modern unscientific use of the word science, we use it in the sense of the physical sciences only and to our peril ignore Spencer's description of theology as "the queen of the sciences". Most of my working life has been given to the consideration of problems of philology and theology and homiletics, set all the while against the background of a consuming interest in people as people—their needs, problems, hopes, fears. Who am I then to address you who specialize, or will shortly do so, in branches of learning far from those which I would like to think are my own—in anatomy, and surgery, chemistry, and psychiatry, and so forth? Perhaps, however, the fact that your spheres of learning and mine are so different from one another may in itself constitute a measure of justification for my speaking to you to-day.

For however much our lines of study may differ, we have one thing in common. It is what I have described as "a consuming interest in people as people". At least if we have not, then the sooner you give over the idea of the practice of medicine, the better; and the sooner I give over the calling of the parson, the better. Heaven help your patient if, as you visit him in home or in hospital, you simply regard him as one more "bod". Heaven help my people, when they come to see me in my study or I visit them in their homes, if I simply regard them as so many "souls". But that is to anticipate.

One of the greatest perils to which our particular age is in danger of succumbing is the peril of over-departmentalization, of exclusive specialization. Let me explain what I mean. The title which I have given to this lecture to doctors and doctors-to-be, "The wholeness of man", might equally well have served as the title of a lecture to educationists. For after all what *is* education? Is it the cramming of the little darling with so many facts that he can successfully defeat the examiners at all stages? Is the educationist concerned to produce walking encyclopaedias even if only in abridged editions? Or is he concerned to help in producing a whole person, nourished and reared (for that is the meaning of *educare*) into fulness of life? These are fundamental questions to which any educationist worth his salt must give his attention.

Or again, my subject might well have been the theme for a lecture to those whose task will be to administer justice. For what is the purpose of the judge in the law-courts? Is it simply to wreak vengeance on the wrong-doer, or is it so to dispense justice that, on the one hand, society may live in safety, and, on the other hand, the criminal may be restored to wholeness of life as an individual and as a member of his community? And what is the purpose of the administrator? Is it simply to suppress anti-social forces by use of the mailed fist? Or is it rather to create and maintain such conditions that a healthy creative community life may flourish? The problem has been pin-pointed for us in recent months by the "Report of the Committee on homosexual offences and prostitution", 1957. Is the law to continue to treat the homosexual as a criminal only, from whom, quite rightly, society must be protected? Or is it so to administer its affairs that the health of the homosexual himself is given at least as great a measure of consideration as is the welfare of the society of which he is a member?

"The wholeness of man"—it is a theme of first importance for the consideration of doctor, of parson, of teacher, of judge. And the task of each of these four people impinges directly, or indirectly, on that of the others, for the simple reason that every one of them is concerned with *man* himself—that tantalizingly complicated creature *man*. Any member of any one of those four callings, if he thinks at all deeply and is not content to be a boor, a mere "hack" at his trade, is bound, sooner or later, to find himself faced by the question "What is man?" It will not then be long before he is faced with further questions, as, for example, the inter-relationship of the medical with the spiritual. He will find that the more he specializes—and there must needs be increasing specialization as knowledge rapidly increases—the more he will need to be alive to the danger of knowing more and more about less and less until he knows everything about nothing at all! That is to exaggerate, but the warning is needed.

If the preacher needs to be warned that it is of little use to preach to men with empty stomachs, the doctor must remember that his patient is more than a body, a conglomeration of chemical compounds. He must be regarded in his totality, in his wholeness. If this is true, then all of us who have anything to do with man and his welfare will have to come to terms with the fact that we shall need more than the amassing of *facts* for the fulfilment of our task: we shall need *wisdom*, a far more elusive thing even than the attainment of knowledge. You may acquire many degrees and become a knowledgeable person, but it is possible that you may not be wise. In so far as that is the case, it is probable that you will fail to—

> Minister to a mind diseas'd,
> Pluck from the memory a rooted sorrow,
> Raze out the written troubles of the brain,
> And with some sweet oblivious antidote
> Cleanse the stuff'd bosom of that perilous stuff
> Which weighs upon the heart.
> (Macbeth. V.3)

You will remember that Macbeth asked the doctor if he could not do just this for Lady Macbeth, tortured as she was in conscience. The doctor replied:

> Therein the patient
> Must minister to himself

—small comfort indeed!

This leads on to a further question. What do we mean by the wholeness of man? Dr. Armand Vincent of Paris quotes a remark made by one of his patients: "We are prevented from dying; we are not helped to live" (quoted by Paul Tournier: *A Doctor's Casebook*, p. 17). Modern medicine has wrought wonders in the sphere of preventing people from dying. The rate of infant mortality has dropped astonishingly; man's longevity has been so increased that there has grown up a science of *geriatrics*, a word unknown at least to the layman until quite recently (and absent from the 1936 edition of the two-volume Oxford English Dictionary though *geratology* is given); modern antibiotic drugs save the lives of millions of men and women every year. We are indeed "prevented from dying"— with resultant problems of immense complexity in food production in relation to world population, in family planning, in dissemination of information about contraception and birth control, especially in areas where the level of illiteracy is high, and so on. I am not complaining at the prevention of death which science is so remarkably achieving; I simply draw attention to the problems which issue, hydra-headed, from such prevention. I am concerned with the second part of the patient's remark: "we are not helped to live". In other words, I bid you ask what is meant by *life* as distinct from mere existence, by health, by wholeness.

We can scarcely improve on the definition given in a publication of the British Medical Association in 1956 entitled "Divine Healing and Co-operation between Doctors and Clergy (Memorandum of evidence submitted by a special committee of the Council of the British Medical Association to the Archbishops' Commission on Divine Healing)". The document says (p. 8): "The words *health*, *wholeness*, and *holiness* are closely linked in origin. Healing may be described as the process by which a living organism, whose functions are disordered, is restored or 'made whole', that is to say, returns to complete functioning." The memorandum then goes on to refer to those "psychogenic disorders including psychosomatic states in which physical symptoms result from emotional disturbances—such as 'nervous' headache due to worry, or 'nervous' indigestion due to anxiety or unrecognized resentment". A distinguished psychiatrist holds that 80 per cent of illness is due to resentment, guilt complexes, etc.—a figure significant enough even if, as is necessarily the case, it is impossible to substantiate it with anything approaching mathematical precision. It is, however, true to record that 44 per cent of our hospital beds are occupied by the mentally afflicted; that only 10 per cent of the mentally sick are in hospital, the other 90 per cent being "heavy-laden", rendered ineffective in life and work, but receiving very little attention except in a few out-patient clinics. It is obvious, then, in the light of these facts, that any one who has to do with man's health will have to go very much deeper than the level simply of his physical welfare.

I believe that we may get much light on our problems if we take a backward look into the insights given us by the great figures in the Hebrew tradition. Our own English culture and civilization is a complicated one, deriving its inspiration from many sources. It is a complex of many strands, of which the three most important are the Hebrew, the Greek and the Roman. We do not go to Jerusalem for art—the Hebrews had none, more is the pity. We go to Athens for our inspiration in that field, as we go to Rome for guidance in the sphere of law and government. Thus, even in the twentieth century, we do not have to define the phrase "the classics". Our minds leap at once to the treasures of Greece and Rome, the writings of Plato and Aeschylus, of Ovid and Cicero. But if you are looking for the deepest insights into the nature of man, his make-up, his function, his destiny, his significance, the nature of his dis-ease, the possibility of his wholeness, then you go to that strand of our complex heritage which is Hebraic in origin and which found highest expression in the writings of the prophets of the Old Testament and in the powerful records of the New. I would submit that we neglect these insights to our peril.

I begin by reminding you of the fundamental realism of the thinking of those ancient writers. A Greek might be content to discuss philosophically and, as it were, in the abstract, the interesting question "Where does evil come from?" Not so the Hebrew. He may have in his literature a primitive story about a man and a woman, a snake and a forbidden fruit. But the point of the story is *not* that it should form the basis for an abstract discussion, along abstract and abstruse philosophical lines, of the origin of evil. The Hebrew was not made that way. He was not a philosopher, sitting on a balcony away above the road of life, viewing it detachedly. He was a practical man, concerned with the agonies of life, its murkiness, its sinfulness, as well as its glory and its beauty. He was puzzled by the contrast between the two sides of life. He was not on the balcony viewing; he was on the road agonizing. *There* he found his insights into truth and reality.

Look for a moment at the old creation story of Genesis. It is to be hoped that, at this time of day, we do not waste our energies in discussing the length of the "days" mentioned in the first chapter, or in trying to play off science against religion or vice-versa! Genesis was not written to give mankind a scientific handbook on the origins of creation. It *does* give mankind, if he is wise enough to see it, profound insights, of paramount importance, into the nature of man as an individual, of man as a partner in the marriage relationship, of man as a member of society. Let me illustrate. The old story paints man as a being set to *work* ("the Lord God took the man, and put him into the garden of Eden to dress it and to keep it"). Man's bliss does not consist in idleness, but in contributing to the welfare of the community—an insight not to be ignored by the many who act as if minimal working hours mean maximum happiness and as if the chief end of man were to escape from labour. The story depicts ideal man as living a life of *limited* freedom. He is *free*—"Of every tree of the garden thou mayest freely eat." But his freedom is *limited*—"Of the tree of the knowledge of good and evil thou shalt not eat." Freedom and licence are not identical. Development needs prohibition, as any gardener will tell you. Expertise can be obtained only by discipline, as any athlete or indeed any master of the art of medicine will tell you. You will find your freedom only when you discover the meaning of limitation and service; as the old Latin prayer had it *"cui servire est regnare"*—"Whom to serve is to reign"—a profoundly true paradox.

Or again, ideal man is depicted as made for fellowship. The male by himself is not self-sufficient. He needs "an help answering to him". Thus the Biblical reader's introduction to what we might call the theology of sexuality is an introduction to something essentially good, God-given, to be welcomed, reverenced and rejoiced in, a thing which, apart from sin, involves no shame, a thing which issues in a union so close that the partners become one flesh, enjoying a "togetherness" which takes precedence even over parental ties. If this view of things sounds to you refreshingly "modern", open, uninhibited, I bid you ask yourself whether the common presentation of the Biblical view of man is the right one. It might be a matter of surprise to some of you to examine the material for yourself; to note the complete and utter frankness of the Old Testament and indeed of the New on matters physical, including the sexual; and the insistence at once on the littleness of man and at the same time on his vast significance. Never does the Bible sink to that view of the body of which Plato wrote in a famous pun—"the body is for us a tomb" of the spirit. No Hebrew could ever subscribe to a view of man which regarded him as a kind of angel in a slot machine, a soul (the invisible, spiritual essential ego) incarcerated in a frame of matter, from which it trusts eventually to be liberated. Sub-Christian hymns may give this impression, but not the Bible. Even St. Paul's "vile body" (Philippians 3 : 21) is a vile translation and a vile misrepresentation of what he meant! We are nearer to the Biblical view of man when we regard him as "flesh animated by the soul, the whole conceived as a psycho-physical unity" (J. A. T. Robinson, *The Body*, p. 14); cf. J. A. C. Murray: "The spirit is the living body seen from within, and the body the outward manifestation of the living spirit" (*Christian Psychotherapy*, pp. 149–50).

It is against that background of the wonder of man, amazing complex that he is of the physical and the spiritual, that the Hebrews pondered on and wrestled with the problem of his wrongness. That there *was* something wrong with individual man and with society was so obvious to them that they did not waste time in debating it. They could never sing with A. C. Swinburne:

> Glory to Man in the highest!
> For Man is the maker of things;

or with W. E. Henley:

> It matters not how strait the gate,
> How charged with punishments the scroll,
> I am the master of my fate:
> I am the captain of my soul

for, as they looked around them, they saw how patently untrue such sentiments are! In fact, the central theme of the whole Bible is essentially that of man's dis-ease and of its cure, as John Milton saw when he entitled his two greatest works "Paradise Lost" and "Paradise Regained".

It is at this point that we are confronted with a very interesting fact. The Hebrew idea of *salvation*, which is perhaps *the* central Biblical idea which holds all the books together, making a heterogeneous library into a unity, derives from a word which means "to be spacious". It is the root behind the name of the old deliverer-judge, Joshua, a name which we know better in its Greek form Jesus. Joshua was an agent in the hand of the God of Israel who, in the Biblical phrase, "wrought salvation" for the people; who, as we say, got them out of a tight corner; who, to revert to Biblical language, set their feet in a large room. It is an interesting concept, this, that man's dis-ease results in the restriction and constriction of his freedom, and fulness of life; he is repressed; he is inhibited. But in saying this, I have slipped into the usage of twentieth-century psychological terms. Is it possible that the Hebrews had insights into man's nature and ills which we are rather belatedly recovering?

It is at least worth looking into a little more closely. This central idea of "salvation" is used as we have seen in a *military* sense—"the Lord wrought salvation for His people" when their enemies were pressing them in. If a Hebrew had been writing up the battles of the last war, he would have said that Montgomery wrought salvation for the Allies when, by some great deployment of forces, he enabled them to make a breakthrough from the trap in which they found themselves. (The aforesaid Hebrew would probably have added that "Monty smote Rommel in the hinder parts"—a pleasant picture!) The idea is also used in a *naval* sense—of the rescue of men's lives which had been imperilled by a great storm at sea. It is also used in a *medical* sense, of the restoration to full health of one whose fulness of life has been impaired by sickness. Thus, in a famous passage in St. Mark (a passage, by the way, in which he is more unkind to the doctors than is Dr. Luke when he is telling the same story!) there is the narrative of a woman who came to Jesus for cure after spending all she had on doctors and finding no improvement in her condition. Her contact with Jesus brings restoration to health. Jesus is recorded as saying to her, "Daughter, your confidence has *saved* you, made you fit; go into peace . . ." (St. Mark 5 : 34). That is to say, for twelve long years you have lived a life cramped and confined by this illness. Now the old restrictions are gone. Previously you have lived in distress and embarrassment. Now you may turn your back on all that, and go into a life of peace and integration.

Such is the Biblical idea of the *wholeness* of man—freedom from all that cramps fulness of life and development; integration; body, mind and spirit working in harmony.

Against that general background, we may turn to the Gospels, briefly to study the picture given there of the way in which Jesus set to work to bring about the wholeness of man. I would draw your attention to four points:

1. Jesus struck a blow at the current Jewish doctrine which viewed suffering as invariably the consequence of sin, either on the part of the sufferer or of his forebears. The clearest case of this is the story of the man born blind recorded in the 9th Chapter of St. John. Life makes it pretty obvious that frequently the proposition that suffering is the result of sin is true. But not invariably. If it be objected that the story gives us no positive philosophy of evil and of suffering, it may be replied that nowhere in the recorded sayings of Jesus is such a philosophy to be found; but, negative though the blow be which the story strikes, it removes at one stroke much of the bitterness which the current theory caused and, it may be added, still causes, in the minds of multitudes.

2. Jesus when faced by physical and mental sickness almost invariably showed Himself a fighter. So far as we can judge from the Gospels, it would appear that for Jesus to be *con*fronted by disease was to be *af*fronted. The Oxford English Dictionary defines "to affront" as to "insult to the face . . . to put to the blush . . . to cause to feel ashamed". Our Lord meets a poor woman with a twisted body (St. Luke 13 : 11). What does

He do? Sigh, and pass by? No. Such a state of things He feels to be an affront to the plan of God, and an insult to His face. "This woman . . . Satan hath bound." He heals her, and she finds her body not a hindrance to the service of God, but an expression of His glory.

Again, St. Mark (1 : 40) gives us the story of the leper who came to Jesus. He records the compassion with which Jesus viewed the pitiable figure. But in a well-known variant reading no compassion is recorded but rather anger. Judging by the canon of textual criticism which lays it down that the more difficult reading is the more likely, it is more probable that Jesus showed anger than compassion according to this story. We may well ask at what or at whom was Jesus thus incensed? Not at the by-standers (as in the story of the healing of the man with the withered hand, St. Mark 3 : 5) for no mention is made of them. Perhaps the anger of Jesus expressed the divine anger against sin, of which leprosy, a living death, spoke. But is it not more likely that the record of this anger is the evangelist's attempt to express the reaction, the shame, which Jesus felt at the utter wrongness of the havoc wrought by sickness on the miracle which is a man's body? These instances—and there are others worthy of careful study—show us One who, so far from showing any resignation to suffering and death, seems to have opposed them with all the power at His command. He was a fighter against those elements in life which detracted from man's fulness of life, from his full health, from his "salvation". I may add in passing that to many of us this second point which I am making would be an indication of the way in which doctors and clergy should work together in the closest possible co-operation in as much as both are involved in an attack on all that cramps man's growth and development and peace.

3. Jesus refused in His healing work to concentrate solely upon the ills of the body. A paralytic is brought on his mattress bed to Jesus (St. Mark 2 : 1). He looks expectantly to Him for physical healing. What must have been his surprise when Jesus said to him, not "Thy paralysis is cured" but "Thy sins are forgiven!" The great Physician diagnosed the trouble which underlay the outward manifestation of it which was the physical paralysis. He saw that if there was to be a complete and

permanent cure, the *whole* man must be dealt with. First, his relationship to God and to his fellows must be put right, then his physical healing would follow and there would go to his house a man every whit whole.

Again, the story of a demon-possessed man, told as it is no doubt only in outline (St. Mark 5 : 1–20), reminds us almost of a modern psychiatrist's approach to his patient. Jesus is apparently at considerable pains to get alongside the deranged man. He sympathetically questions him—"What is thy name?" and elicits the significant answer of what sounds like a schizophrenic: "My name is Legion: for we are many." After the cure, Doctor and patient are together, presumably in close conclave ("They came to Jesus and saw him that was possessed —sitting"). Mere expulsion of the demons was not enough. The man must feel that he is understood. He must be made whole in the totality of his personality.

The importance of this point can hardly be exaggerated. Any "healing movement" which simply goes out to cure physical sickness without reference to the well-being of the whole personality will have results compared with which the efforts of a bull in a china shop will be pacific. For if, as we have seen, it is true that suffering is not *invariably* the consequence of sin, it is also equally true that time and time again suffering is the manifestation in the physical part of him of a man's maladjustment to God, to his environment, or to himself. To attempt to cure the symptom without dealing with the root of the problem is like putting on a new tile to the roof when the foundations of the building are totally inadequate. When Jesus healed a man's or a woman's body or mind, that healing was one of the ways, one of the most expressive and eloquent ways, in which the Love of God in Him went out to folk in need. But the God who made man as a psychosomatic unity loves that man in his entirety, and, if we may say so reverently, is all out for his total restoration. It was a wise French clinician who said: "Il n'y a pas des maladies, seulement les malades" ("there are no sicknesses, only sick people").

4. Jesus' greatest contribution in the realm of suffering was not what He did in healing, nor what He taught by word, but what He was in His person. The picture which the early

documents give of Jesus is not of some superb Apollo, though it may be noted that we have no record of the sickness of Jesus but have, rather, the impression of one perfectly integrated and supremely at peace with God and with Himself. Rather do the documents stress the fact that He whose name was Immanuel entered into our griefs with a terrible intimacy. St. Matthew, after recording Christ's healing of a leper, of the centurion's servant, of Peter's mother-in-law, and of the demon-possessed, concludes the section by recalling the words of Isaiah and noting their fulfilment in our Lord: "Himself took our infirmities and bare our sicknesses" (St. Matthew 8: 17). He was indeed, as He Himself taught, the suffering Servant foreshadowed in the great Isaianic prophecies. It is the function of the *servants* in society to carry the burdens and to do the dirty work of mankind. Here, it seems to me, we have a strong suggestion that any one who is to get to grips with man's sickness needs more than technical skill, more even than a "bedside manner"; needs, indeed, a measure of that sympathy which means literally *suffering* with the person concerned. This, I need hardly remind you, entails a ministry, whether in medicine or in psychiatry or in the pastoral work of the Church, which is a very costly thing. It means, in short, taking a large share of other people's loads on yourself, and it is doubtful whether much permanently worthwhile work can be done without precisely this.

I would express the hope that some, particularly of the younger members of my audience to-day, may have glimpsed the magnitude of the task which faces anyone who assays to alleviate and cure man's radical dis-ease. Perhaps it has made you tremble at the prospect ahead of you. If so, that is all to the good.

I would hope that what I have tried to say may at least have been a pointer to the fact that, in the mighty assault on man's malaise which is constantly called for, the closest and deepest liaison is needed between doctors and clergy. Gone for ever, I trust, are the days when the Church eyed the man of science with suspicion; when the discoveries of science were thought to clash with the tenets of the Church as though God were not the author of *all* truth, whether it be about the Incarnation or the atom, about the Atonement or the electron. Gone for ever are such days as those when, Galileo's discoveries clashing with the then static views of the Church on cosmogony, a Doctor of the Church, gently altering one letter in a proper name, preached on the text: "Ye men of Galileo, why stand ye gazing up into heaven?" And gone, too, one hopes, are the days when science, over-sure in the abundance of her discoveries, looked across at the Church and said: "We have no need of you." Such a sentiment belongs more to the first decade of this century than to the present decade. All of us realize more to-day how radical is man's dis-ease than did our fathers. Many of us have glimpsed the imperative need of a united assault on a common enemy. It is significant that, as recently as 1919, the term "psychosomatic medicine" was unknown to the medical vocabulary. The now current use of this compound word is indicative of a far-reaching change in the approach of medicine towards the cause and treatment of disease. An immense amount of research and study and conference is going on between the best minds in medicine and in theology and religion, as a reading of *The Church's Ministry of Healing* (Report of the Archbishops' Commission, 1958) will show.

Twenty-five years have passed since Jung wrote in a well-known passage: "Among my patients in the second half of life—that is to say, over thirty-five—there has not been one whose problem in the last resort was not that of finding a religious outlook on life. It is safe to say that every one of them fell ill because he had lost that which the living religions of every age have given to their followers, and none of them has been really healed who did not regain his religious outlook" (*Modern Man in Search of a Soul*, p. 264). Jung comments: "It is indeed high time for the clergyman and the psychotherapist to join forces to meet this great spiritual task" (p. 265).

Such joining of forces has in large measure taken place and is taking place between scientists and theologians of top rank. But if the wholeness of man is to be worked out in any enduring way in the highways and byways of our island, not to mention the teeming under-privileged populations of vast countries overseas, it will happen only as general practitioner Dr. Jones and Vicar Smith work together, and maybe pray together, about John Brown who is ill and whom they would see *whole*.

14

PARENTS WHO DON'T CARE ENOUGH

From *The Sunday Telegraph*, December 24, 1961

14

IN FRONT OF me on my desk lie two articles which have greatly interested me. One, from a famous newspaper, is written by a mother who is complaining at the rift which has grown between her twenty-year-old daughter and herself. She says that she and her husband have contrived to give this daughter everything to make her comfortable and happy, even to the point of luxury; but now—a barrier, a rift!

I looked to see what place religion had occupied in the bringing up of this girl. The only reference I could find was that it had been "discussed quite freely", together with sex, politics, and current affairs.

The other article was printed in one of the monthly digests. It consisted of twelve "rules for parents who wish to turn their children into juvenile delinquents". It was written by the Police Department of a great city. The third rule ran: "Never give him any spiritual training. Wait until he is twenty-one, and then let him 'decide for himself'." The article ended: "Prepare for a life of grief. You will be likely to have it."

The researches which *Inquirer* has been conducting in "what the churches are doing" have been summarized in these columns [in the *Sunday Telegraph*] over the past months; and very illuminating they have been. He has been encouraged by very much of what he has seen of the impact which the Church is making through the Chaplain in a factory or holiday resort, through the padre in a hospital or big department store, and through the ordinary layman working in a Youth Club, welcoming overseas students or foreign seamen, and so on. He has been especially impressed by the work of the Church among young people, and by their response—in churches, in schools, and in universities. In some cases it is the young people who lead their parents back to a vital faith. I would corroborate this last point, for, during nearly six years as a bishop, I have found a large number of adults, often men and women in middle life, coming forward to Confirmation. Not seldom is that due to the fact that they see their youngsters with a religion which "ticks", a religion which hitherto they themselves have never had.

But—and here *Inquirer* has a warning which we shall do well to consider very carefully—the writer of the articles in these columns says that it is clear that those who in schools and universities have looked at the Church and rejected it are in a large majority. He pinpoints the reason for this. Nearly always, he says, *this indifference only mirrors that in the young people's own homes.* Too often the seed sown in school or university or home church falls on stony ground.

That analysis of the contemporary situation is one which only a fool will dismiss without further careful thought. "Never give him any spiritual training. Wait until he is twenty-one, and then let him 'decide for himself' "—so said the police, and they know a thing or two. *Spiritual training*—note the phrase they use with reference to parents and their children. This is something the responsibility for which cannot be put on to the schoolteachers or even the clergy. They can do a certain amount, but their influence is strictly limited. It is the home influence which counts. Nor can a bit of family church-going at Christmas or Easter or some other big occasion pretend to be spiritual training. Spiritual training involves the catching of a habit by the child from the parents. Religion is caught as well as taught. The youngster who is *sent* to church rather than accompanied to church will soon give up the habit, arguing that church-going is one of those things you grow out of at sixteen—"after all, look at Dad!" Can you blame him?

If some of us cared for the physical welfare of our young people as little as we do for their spiritual health, they would have been dead long ago. If some of us cared for the mental welfare of our young people as little as we do for their spiritual health, they would have been illiterate—or we should have been locked up for neglecting their education. And yet, in thousands of British homes to-day, our children are being trained in hygiene of the body, given expensive clothing, entertainment and education, but—*spiritual training*? Here there is almost total neglect. And the youngsters grow up—only to find that, when the testing times come, they have no inner resources with which to meet them.

On the other hand, experience goes to show that "the family that prays together stays together"; and that the youngster who grows up to enjoy a healthy religion which is as natural a part of his training as are the other activities which he regularly shares with his parents has a foundation for life which stands the stresses and strains.

The parent who really cares for the welfare of his child will ponder *Inquirer's* findings—and take action, even though such action may call for a pretty radical re-shaping of personal and family life. But that way he will avoid that condition which a writer in *The Listener* some time back described thus: "A condition in which Things take precedence over Thought, in which personal indulgence is put above general good, in which a fatty layer is grown around conscience, in which change, adventure, and risk are above all feared."

15

A GUIDING INFLUENCE FOR OVER THREE CENTURIES

From *The Times* Supplement on the Bible in English, March 27, 1961

15

THIRTEEN HUNDRED YEARS is a long time in the growth of a nation. But it is impossible to speak about the influence of the English Bible on the life and character, the literature and thought of the English people without going back at least that far. True, the outlines of history are dim and the facts not easily verifiable when one is dealing with the seventh century A.D.; but it seems probable that there is truth in the story that just about 1,300 years ago a labourer at the monastery of Whitby, who later became a monk there, turned much of the Scriptures into verse as a result of a vision vouchsafed to him. So Caedmon became the first Anglo-Saxon writer of popular religious poetry, though it is likely that even before his time there were paraphrases from the Latin scriptures into the vernacular. A country like Britain, which could as early as 314 send three of its own bishops to the Council of Arles, presumably had considerable parts of the Scriptures in its own common language.

Perhaps the best way of surveying what is a very long stretch of history and a vast subject will be to focus the light of our inquiry on certain people and on incidents of particular interest. To put it another way, we shall flash on the screen of our mind a short series of pictures that will illustrate our theme.

The first we have already glanced at—Caedmon who, so the old story goes, felt keenly his inability to sing and, when he saw the harp coming his way at the monastery at Whitby, would leave the table. But one night when he had done so, and had lain down in the stable and there fallen asleep, there stood One by him in a dream, and said, "Caedmon, sing Me something." And he answered, "I cannot sing, and for that reason I have left the feast." But He said, "Sing the beginning of created things." So he sang; and the poem of Caedmon is the first native growth of English literature.

Our second picture comes again from the north of England.

This time it is Jarrow and the date is 735. The Venerable Bede tells us that he spent all his years in the Jarrow monastery, "ever intent upon the study of the Scriptures. In the intervals between the duties enjoined by the disciplinary rule and the daily care of chanting in the church, I took sweet pleasure in always learning, teaching or writing". Now it is Ascension Day, 735, and Bede is on his death bed. Let his faithful disciple Cuthbert tell us the story of the finishing of the translation of St. John's Gospel. "In the evening his boy-scribe said to him, 'One sentence, dear master, is left unfinished.' He bade him write quickly. Soon the boy announced that it was finished. 'True,' the dying man said, 'it is finished. Take mine head between thy hands and raise me. Full fain would I sit with my face to my holy oratory, where I was ever wont to pray, that sitting so I may call on my Father.' And so he sat on the floor of his cell, and chanted 'Glory be to the Father and to the Son and to the Holy Ghost.' And as he breathed the words 'the Holy Ghost', he died." So the good work of the translation of Scripture into a language that the common people could understand went on.

Centuries pass, and we go for our third picture to Lutterworth in Leicestershire, the scene of the work and ministry of John Wyclif. Some forty-four years after his death in 1384, the Pope ordered the Bishop of Lincoln "to proceed in person to the place where John Wycliffe was buried, cause his body and bones to be exhumed, cast far from ecclesiastical burial and publicly burnt, and his ashes to be so disposed of that no trace of him shall be seen again."

The offence, for which this dire penalty was prescribed, was that Wyclif had unlocked the Bible to the common English reader. "Thus," wrote the old historian Thomas Fuller, "this brook"—he is referring to the River Swift—"hath conveyed his ashes into Avon; Avon into Severn; Severn into the narrow seas; they into the main ocean. And thus the ashes of Wyclif are the emblem of his doctrine, which now is dispersed all the world over." The claim is scarcely exaggerated. It is indeed a fact that only part of the Wyclif Bible is actually the work of John Wyclif himself—Nicholas Hereford at Oxford translated much of the Old Testament. But the impetus was Wyclif's, and the whole work appeared two years before his death. It was, as G. M. Trevelyan has said, "an admirable and scholarly piece of work, a great event in the history of the English language as well as religion." Wyclif was a man before his time, one of those

> deathless minds which leave when they have past
> A path of light.

Indeed, the light was needed, for it was a day when many of the clergy could not construe or expound the Lord's Prayer, nor the creed or the ten commandments. The plight of the laity must have been dire; and it is deeply significant that the copies of the Wyclif Bible still extant are small, unadorned, and closely written, indicating that they were meant not for the mighty and the wealthy but for the man in the street.

In the year 1477 Caxton set up his press under the shadow of Westminster Abbey. What a weapon this was to be for the dissemination of literature and in particular of the English Bible! No longer would it be necessary laboriously to copy out each gospel or epistle by hand. Wyclif's Bible of the previous century, or Tyndale's of the ensuing one, would be rolled off in their hundreds and thousands of copies by this stupendous invention.

Before we come to Tyndale we ought to glance at Oxford around the year 1500. There we see a young man just back from Italy, full of the heady knowledge of the Renaissance. The ancient classics had come alive for him. But it is not on these that he is lecturing. It is on the Epistles of St. Paul. His lecture room is crowded to the doors. John Colet, close friend of Erasmus and of Sir Thomas More, is bringing these old letters to life in a way that Oxford had never known before. The great doctrines are seen to be not the relics of an age gone by nor the property of the schoolmen only, but the word of God for every man who has ears to hear them. The expository skill of Colet at Oxford, of Erasmus at Cambridge and of many who lit their lamps from the fire of their learning—this, married to the technical skill of Caxton and his successors, put the Bible unfettered into the hands of the English people.

For our next picture we turn to William Tyndale, whose life and work (and, it should be added, his martyr-death) are of inestimable importance in the story of the English Bible. It has been reckoned that 90 per cent of Tyndale's translation stands unaltered in the Authorized Version of 1611. No wonder that Professor Greenslade can call him "the man who more than Shakespeare even or Bunyan has moulded and enriched our language". This man, driven by a great passion to "cause a boy that driveth the plough to know more of the Scripture" than did many of the clergy of the day, had an uncanny gift of lifting the common language, in a true nobility of homeliness, up to the sublime level of the Bible. When, as we read the pages of the Authorized Version, we find ourselves moved by such a phrase as "until the day dawn and the day-star arise in our hearts"; or "in Him we live and move and have our being"; or "for here we have no continuing city but we seek one to come", we are, whether we realize it or not, indebted to William Tyndale. Driven out by persecution from London, Tyndale did his greatest work on the Continent, whence copies of his translation were smuggled out, some in bales of cotton and some by other surreptitious means, into this country. In 1536 he was martyred by strangulation and burning. His last prayer was "Lord, open the King of England's eyes." Little did he dream that that prayer was to be answered in the very next year by the royal recognition of the Coverdale Bible, which itself was enormously indebted to Tyndale's.

We pass by Coverdale's work, with only a glance of thankfulness for that lovely version of the Psalms that is enshrined as a monument to him in our Prayer Book, and with, perhaps, a touch of regret that such a rendering as "There is no more triacle at Galaad" (Jeremiah 8:22) never found its way into the Authorized Version. And so we come, for our last picture, to 1611. Or, rather, to 1604, for it was in that year, the year after the death of Queen Elizabeth I, that at the Hampton Court Conference, with the full approval and encouragement of King James I, a new translation was decided on. The King James version (or, as it is known to us, though less accurately, the Authorized Version) is the final answer to those who maintain that no good thing can come out of the deliberations of a committee.

This version was the result of the work of a committee, itself divided into six sub-committees, two sitting at Westminster, two at Oxford and two at Cambridge. The members were the cream of the scholarship of the day. It was said, for example, of Bishop Launcelot Andrewes, who headed the Westminster group, that "he might have been interpreter general at Babel . . . the world wanted learning to know how learned he was". But the committee was marked not only by culture and learning—it was marked also by humility and piety. In the "Preface of the Translators", the members wrote, rather delightfully: "We never thought from the beginning, that we should need to make a new Translation, nor yet to make of a bad one a good one . . . but to make a good one better, or out of many good ones, one principal good one, not justly to be excepted against: that hath been our endeavour, that our mark."

It is easy to look back from the vantage point of the passage of 350 years and to detect errors in scholarship that the researches of later years have brought to light. We know much more to-day about the Hebrew language and about Greek manuscripts than did Launcelot Andrewes and his colleagues. But I think that Macaulay was right when he described the 1611 version as "a book which, if everything else in our language should perish, would alone suffice to show the whole extent of its beauty and power".

It was a matter of extreme good fortune that the King James version came into being just when it did, for this was the period when our language reached what G. M. Trevelyan has called "its brief perfection". It was the age of Shakespeare and Marlowe, of Spenser, Hooker and Bacon. There is a kind of monosyllabic simplicity and yet majesty about much of the language. Consider this: "Thus will I bless Thee while I live: I will lift up my hands in Thy name." Or: "The Son of Man is come to seek and to save that which was lost." Or again: "The flowers appear on the earth; the time of the singing of birds is come, and the voice of the turtle is heard in our land." For sheer beauty, it would be hard to improve on sentences such as these. It was this kind of English that fixed the standard for centuries to come.

It was hard to improve—impossible perhaps—on the language of the Bible and the Prayer Book and of Shakespeare.

There had been a steady progress and enrichment from Chaucer to Elizabeth, and the peak point was reached in the early years of the seventeenth century. Even to-day, three and a half centuries later, our common speech is vastly enriched by the cadences and proverbs of this version. Very often those who use such phrases as "the skin of my teeth", "heap coals of fire on his head", "the fat of the land", "the salt of the earth", "the powers that be", "the pearl of great price", "hip and thigh", do not realize to what an extent they are indebted to this most formative of all translations.

I have spoken of the influence of the Bible on our English speech. But as a matter of fact, it had an influence far deeper on our character, on our religion, and on our social history. In a famous sentence, J. R. Green wrote of the time of Queen Elizabeth I: "England became the people of a book and that book was the Bible." G. M. Trevelyan, who perhaps better than any other living Englishman has described our social history, says that "when Elizabeth came to the throne, the Bible and Prayer Book formed the intellectual and spiritual foundation of a new social order." "For every Englishman who had read Sidney or Spenser, or had seen Shakespeare acted at the Globe, there were hundreds who had read or heard the Bible with close attention as the word of God. The effect of the continual domestic study of the book upon the national character, imagination and intelligence for nearly three centuries to come, was greater than that of any literary movement in our annals, or any religious movement since the coming of St. Augustine." That is a stupendous claim, but it is one that can be amply justified. Let us look at two illustrations.

Some sixty or seventy years after the 1611 version appeared, a tinker in Bedford was writing prose of extraordinary power. His education had been very slight, his reading limited mainly to the Bible, the Book of Common Prayer, and Foxe's Book of Martyrs. John Bunyan's most famous book, *The Pilgrim's Progress*, opens like this: "I dreamed and behold I saw a man clothed with rags, standing in a certain place, with his face from his own house, a Book in his hand, and a great burden upon his back. I looked, and saw him open the book and read therein; and as he read, he wept and trembled; and not being able longer to contain, he broke out with a lamentable cry, saying 'What shall I do?' " "A Book in his hand"—that was true not only of John Bunyan but of tens of thousands of his fellow-countrymen. The days were long past when they had to be dependent on the mystery plays for a knowledge of the drama of Biblical events, or on strolling preachers such as the lollards, or on a visit to the local church to read from a Bible chained to the lectern. The Bible was available to practically every man, and available in lucid English. "A man, with a book in his hand", from which he learnt the secret of forgiveness and of life —this was an apt description of multitudes from the early decades of the seventeenth century on.

My second illustration is drawn from an engraving. The scene of Edward Prentis's "Evening Prayer" is set in a middle-class home of about 1850. The table has been cleared except for a vase of flowers. At the table sits the head of the house, a book open in front of him. His glasses are on, and he is reading to the family, including a small child and an old lady with her work-basket beside her. Near the door sit the maid and a working man. There is no question what the book is. It is the Bible which in this way, by daily reading and pondering, became a powerful influence in tens of thousands of homes. A nation's character was largely moulded not only by what was heard in church, but by what was read and reverently listened to at home.

I have tried in this article to indicate something of the power the English Bible has exercised on the life and character, the language and literature of our people. It is small wonder, against that background, that when at the Coronation Service the Archbishop of Canterbury presents a Bible to the sovereign he says: "Most gracious King, we present you with this Book, the most valuable thing that this world affords. Here is wisdom, this is the royal law; these are the lively oracles of God."

16

FACING THE WORLD'S NEED

An address delivered to the Third Assembly of the World Council of Churches, New Delhi, December 1, 1961

16

WHEN THE INFANT Church of Jesus Christ went out into the world, it went with a book in its hand. That book was what we now call the Old Testament. The Church had good authority for taking such equipment. Jesus Christ Himself, on the occasion of His first sermon in His home town, had read from Isaiah 61 and had said, "This day is this Scripture fulfilled in your ears" (St. Luke 4:21). The risen Lord had expounded to the two disciples on the road to Emmaus "the things concerning Himself in all the Scriptures" (St. Luke 24:27). No wonder that the early Church was a Church with a book in its hand.

It has been so all down the years—only the book in the early days of the Church became a book of two Testaments. Very early in its history, the Church had to come to terms with the task of translating those Scriptures into the tongues of the peoples to which it went. Hence the Versions which are now everyday tools of Biblical scholars. We need not concern ourselves here with those early efforts. What interests us is what we may call *the Bible Society Movement*, which in England began in 1804, that exciting period of Church history which saw the beginning of the modern missionary movement in the birth of great societies for the propagation of the Gospel by word of mouth and by literature. Something of what has been achieved during the last 150–160 years may be seen by a glance at chart I. Before the Bible Society movement began, the number of languages in which the Scriptures had been published was 71. It is now 1,165. And that represents languages spoken by about 95 per cent of the world's population. That is a story of glorious achievement. But before we begin to rest on our oars with even these figures before us, let us remember three things:

(1) that in many of those 1,165 languages only *parts* of the Bible have been translated;

135

CHART I

1100 UP!

The Holy Scriptures have already been published (in whole or in part) in over 1,150 languages

NUMBER OF LANGUAGES

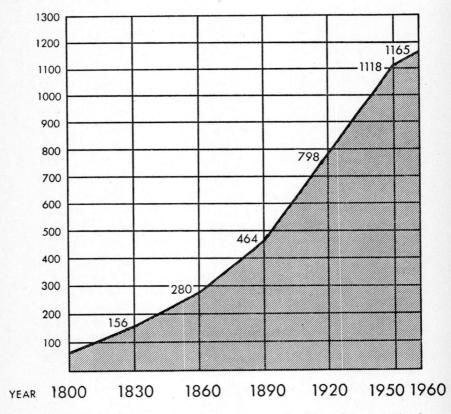

The 1960 total represents languages spoken by about 95% of the world's population.

There are still over 1,000 languages, mutually unintelligible, in which some parts at least of the Scriptures should be translated.

(2) that there are still over a thousand languages, mutually
unintelligible, in which some parts at least of the Bible
should be translated;
(3) that many of these translations desperately need radical
attention and revision, in the interests of accuracy and
"meaningfulness". Many were made by men whose
zeal and devotion were unrivalled, but whose knowledge of the relevant languages was severely limited.

Here is a matter of considerable urgency for the Christian
Church. If the edge of the Church's weapon is not to be blunted
by inaccuracy and even error, the Church must be prepared
gladly to set aside its best men and women, even at great cost
to other departments of its work, to do this task which calls for
technical skill, delicacy of touch, and spiritual insight.

The times are propitious for advance in the translation and
distribution of the Bible and of aids to its understanding. The
days of minute critical Biblical analysis in which many of us
were brought up thirty to forty years ago have led to a "syn-
thetic" approach, which enables us to speak with confidence of
"the message" of the New Testament or of the Bible. There has
been a Biblical renewal in the last half century. If I mention the
names of Karl Barth, of C. H. Dodd and of Reinhold Niebuhr,
it is but to choose three from different nations and traditions
who have contributed much to such a renewal. Nor is this
renewal of interest confined to the circles of scholarship. Much
has percolated down to the man in the street. Evangelistic
campaigns such as those of Dr. Billy Graham have done much
to extend the influence of such movements as the Bible Reading
Fellowship and of the Scripture Union, and of Bible corre-
spondence courses (in India alone during the last ten years more
than half a million people, mainly non-Christians, have enrolled
in such courses).

Nor is this renewal confined to the non-Roman world. Under
Roman Catholic influence, translations have recently been
made in many European languages. One thinks, for example, of
six new ones in France since the war, and of the influential
translation of Ronald Knox made with the approval of the
Roman Catholic hierarchy in England.

CHART 2

1200 MILLION

World Scripture circulation by Bible Societies in twentieth century

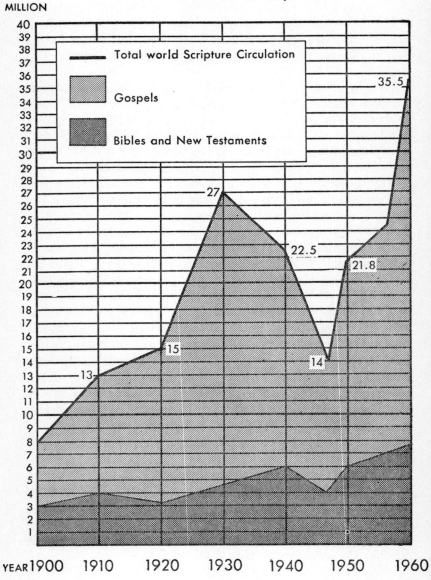

Outside the churches, however, there is a rising interest in the Bible and in things Biblical. If this interest is sometimes rather superficial it is not to be despised. The finds at Qumran have caught the popular imagination. The Press makes much of Biblical archaeology. Visitors to the recent Brussels Exhibition saw the Bible exhibited in more than a dozen pavilions. Hollywood and other film-making centres are not afraid to put on films with such titles as "The Queen of Sheba", "King of Kings", "David and Bathsheba", "The Ten Commandments", "The Big Fisherman". By themselves these things may not amount to much. Cumulatively they point to something of a revival of Biblical interest, and for that we may be thankful.

A glance at chart 2 will show you the rise, fiercely interrupted by two world wars, in Scripture circulation by Bible Societies (commercial concerns are left out) since the beginning of this century. The dark grey refers to Bibles and New Testaments, the light grey to Gospels only, the black line to total world Scripture circulation.

If you are interested in figures you may care to know that in the first few months of its publication over two and a half million copies of the New English Bible (New Testament) were sold. Phillips's translation of the New Testament (whole New Testaments and separate parts) has found three and a half million buyers, and Knox's over two million. The Revised Standard Version figures run to nearly nine million Bibles and over four million New Testaments. These are very high figures. What do they amount to? A rosy picture?—one might think so if it were not for two other facts of immense importance. To these we now turn.

I. *The Population Explosion*

No other word is adequate to describe what is happening in these decades, to the deep concern both of the scientist who looks to man's need for physical sustenance, and of the Christian who cares for his spiritual want. A glance at chart 3 will indicate the meteoric rise in world population in these decades in which we live. Two things must be said by way of explanation of this chart. First, the figures are in millions. Secondly, the figures for A.D. 1980 and 2000 are of course estimates only, and

CHART 3

THE CHURCH IN THE WORLD

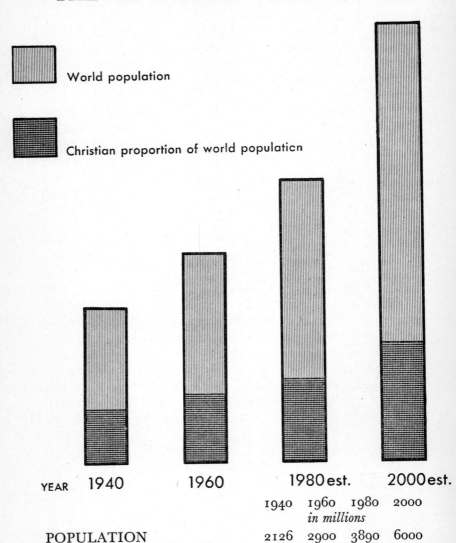

World population

Christian proportion of world population

YEAR	1940	1960	1980 est.	2000 est.

	1940	1960	1980	2000
			in millions	
POPULATION	2126	2900	3890	6000
NUMBER OF CHRISTIANS	692	899	1169	1520

do not allow for any major catastrophe, such as atomic war on a vast scale. They are, however, as near as it is scientifically possible to estimate them. These figures show an increase in world population from two thousand one hundred and twenty-six million (2,126,000,000) in 1940, to six thousand million (6,000,000,000) in A.D. 2000—a fantastic rate of growth in much less than an average white man's lifetime.

There is a further disconcerting factor about this chart. It indicates that there is a decline in the rate of Christian population as compared with that of world population. Thus in 1940 Christians were about 33 per cent of world population. By 1960 they had dropped to 31 per cent. If that rate of decline continues, by A.D. 2000 they will be only 20 per cent. Put that another way and we may say that Christian population is growing one-third as quickly as world population. That discrepancy increases as the rate of world population increases. One could break down those figures for you, but that would be to invite a yawn at this time of day. Let me only add this: these figures, sombre and in some sense menacing as they are, are the best that scientific reckoning can produce. I need not remind an assembly such as this that Almighty God is not subject to the statisticians. There is a Holy Spirit who "bloweth where he listeth" and who has a way of breaking into history unexpectedly when we do need Him most!

II. *The Growth of Literacy*

The second great factor which we must take into consideration is *the growth of literacy*. Every year that passes sees vast numbers of new readers, and those not only children. If I mention Dr. Frank Laubach with his motto "Each one, teach one", I refer certainly to one of the most influential men in this century who have given themselves to the spread of literacy, but I refer to only one among many. One of the first things that the Christian Church has done on going to an unevangelized area is to teach the people to read. The Church has struck a spark which has kindled into a flame which is now a raging forest fire. There is a passion to read—in Asia, in Africa, throughout countries which are still predominantly illiterate. This is true among adults; and the problems facing those

CHART 4

40 CHILDREN — ONE GOSPEL

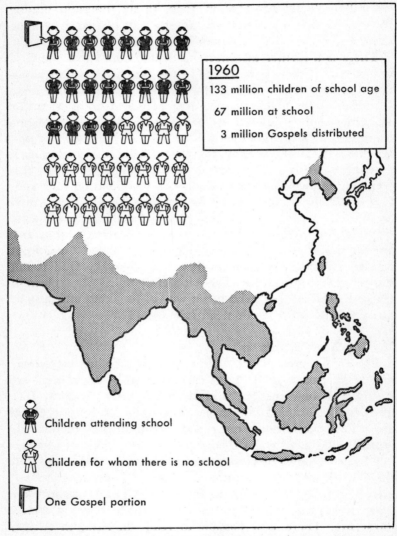

1960
133 million children of school age
67 million at school
3 million Gospels distributed

Children attending school

Children for whom there is no school

One Gospel portion

Based on data supplied by all countries of Asia from Korea to Iran, except China and Japan.

responsible for the education of the young are colossal. How can teachers be found to satisfy the craving for education? Where should the teachers be trained? Which comes first, the provision of teachers or the building of schools?—and so on. It is estimated that in Africa to-day a hundred million adults cannot read. But—quite apart from the "attack from the top", as we might call adult education—"the attack from the bottom", i.e. provision of universal primary education, will add seventeen million new readers from primary schools in that continent by 1970.

What shall they read? On what shall their minds and souls be fed? Salacious literature?—there are not lacking those who would provide it. Communist propaganda?—that is being poured into newly literate areas in vast quantities. Christian good news?—that is one of the greatest challenges of the day.

Let us break the problem down for a moment and limit our survey to one bit of the world. Let us look at all the countries of Asia, from Korea to Iran, excluding China and Japan (chart 4). The date is 1960. One hundred and thirty-three million (133,000,000) children are of school age. Of these, primary schools exist for sixty-seven million (67,000,000). But the number of Gospels distributed in the area was only three million (3,000,000)—one Gospel to forty children!

Have I worried you with too many figures? I will give you only one more chart, which may serve to show the kind of challenge by which the Christian Church throughout the world is confronted. Chart 5 shows that Bible circulation has, during the decades of this century, failed to keep pace with the increase of population. If this is so thus far in the century, what is to happen as the population expansion continues and as literacy increases?

These charts, these figures, these facts of world need, constitute in my opinion a call to the Church to get its priorities right. I end with two questions.

(1) In the strategy of the Church, is anything like enough stress being laid on Christian literature, in view of the rise of literacy and the menace of anti-Christian literary propaganda?

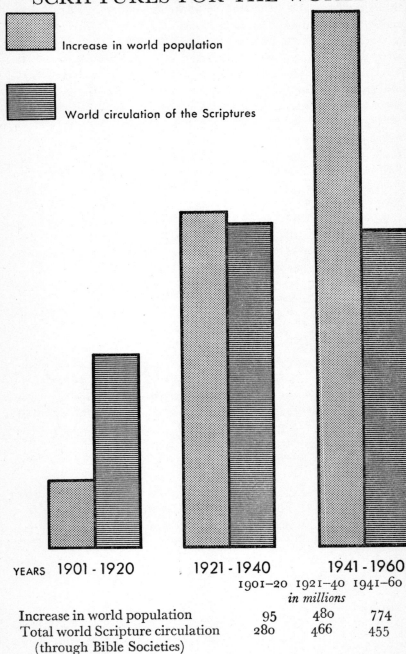

CHART 5

SCRIPTURES FOR THE WORLD?

Increase in world population

World circulation of the Scriptures

	YEARS 1901-1920	1921-1940	1941-1960

	1901-20	1921-40	1941-60
		in millions	
Increase in world population	95	480	774
Total world Scripture circulation (through Bible Societies)	280	466	455

I have a suspicion that by and large it would be true to say that the Church pays lip service to the importance of this work but is not giving itself to the provision of Christian literature at all levels of culture with anything like the care and abandon with which it has pursued the task of, say, medical missions. Yet no less skill and devotion are called for—skill in linguistics, and devotion in understanding the thought forms of the people for whom the literary work is being done. I am not denying the splendid attempts which are being made—one thinks, for example, of Bishop Stephen Neill's series of *World Christian Books*.[1] But the work is pathetically small and hampered on all hands by lack of funds and of that particular expertise which is demanded. Is it possible that, as conditions lead to withdrawal of missionary personnel from many areas, God is calling His Church to the tackling of the task of providing literature on a scale which we have never attempted before?

My second question is more restricted in its range but it brings us back to the particular theme of this meeting:

(2) In the strategy of the Church, are those handmaids of the Church—the Bible Societies—enjoying the support which they deserve, support in skilled manpower and in finance?

If the answer is no, then the challenge comes to us forcefully to look to our priorities lest we go to our warfare either with weapons totally inadequate in number for the task, or with weapons so blunted by the passing of the years that they fail to do the job for which they were made.

[1] Published by the United Society for Christian Literature (Lutterworth Press) and Association Press, New York.

17

UNDER-ESTIMATED THEOLOGICAL BOOKS

P. T. Forsyth's *Positive Preaching and the Modern Mind*
From *The Expository Times*, August, 1961

17

ORE THAN HALF a century has passed since this book
first saw the light of day. Messrs. Hodder and Stoughton
printed it in 1907. My copy, bought in 1949, has the
bookseller's pencilled note: "Scarce. 7s. 6d." Did ever a man
spend 7s. 6d. to better advantage than I did when I bought this
book?

It bears the mark of the age which gave it birth. It reflects
the theological conflicts of its day and the particular Church
allegiance of its distinguished author. The chapters show that
they are lectures (the Lyman Beecher Lecture on Preaching at
Yale University) delivered to ministers in training. All that is
to be expected and it detracts but little from the value of the
book. It is dedicated—in Greek—"unto Him who loved me
and gave Himself for me". That is significant. And the Preface
contains these words: "It has cost the writer much to find his
way so far. And he has yet a long way to go. But he believes
he has found the true and magnetic North."

If you are looking for a book which can be mastered with
little thought and which makes no demands on the reader, do
not take up *Positive Preaching and the Modern Mind*. If you think
that the day of preaching is over and that a little homily of the
newspaper-leader-plus-a-dash-of-religion type will do, do not
take up *Positive Preaching and the Modern Mind*—unless, indeed,
you are prepared for a shattering experience and a mighty
humbling. For this is a book which, like the Word of which it
speaks so much, is "living and powerful, and *pierces*". But will
there ever be great preaching in the Church until the praters
are pierced?

I venture to say that if the first three pages of this book were
digested, believed, worked out and acted on by the men in all
our theological colleges to-day, there would ensue a revolution
in the ministry and the pulpit work of to-morrow's clergy. We
have only reached the second paragraph of the first page when

we are told, fairly and squarely, that preaching is "part of the cultus, and not a mere appendix". "Of course", you say, "nothing new in that." But how many books on preaching deal in any deep way with preaching as itself an act of worship, in which act both preacher and congregation share? In actual fact, is it not the case that in theological colleges, preaching is still the Cinderella of the course? In actual fact, is it not the case that our people—yes, our regular church-goers—often know no better than to regard preaching as "a man talking"? In actual fact, is it not the case that many who have thought out a sacramental theology have not thought out a theology of the Word? We have not got far into the first chapter before we find Forsyth defining grace thus—God's "undeserved and un-bought pardon and redemption of us in the face of our sin, in the face of the world-sin, under such moral conditions as are prescribed by His revelation of His holy love in Jesus Christ and Him crucified". That in itself is enough to give us pause. But Forsyth goes on to relate this to the activity of preaching. The gospel of grace is an act—not a doctrine, a promise, a book, but God's *act* of redemption, an objective power, a historic act and perennial energy of the holy love of God in Christ. "And it is *this act that is prolonged in the word of the preacher*, and not merely proclaimed. The great, the fundamental, sacrament is the Sacrament of the Word" (p. 6: italics mine).

Small wonder, then, that Forsyth contrasts with startling clarity the orator and the preacher—the *orator* having for his business to make real and urgent the present world and its crises; the *preacher* a world unseen, and the whole crisis of the two worlds. The preacher is in the succession of the Hebrew prophets. Engaged on preaching, he is engaged on *the gospel prolonging and declaring itself*.

Preaching as part of the cultus—that is laid down on the first page of the first chapter. And it is elaborated in the truly great chapter, the third, entitled: "The Preacher and his Church, or Preaching as Worship". The temptation to quote at length is strong, but these brief sentences must suffice: "The real presence of Christ crucified is what makes preaching. It is what makes of a speech a sermon, and of a sermon Gospel. This is the work of God, this continues His work in Christ . . .

Every true sermon, therefore, is a sacramental time and act. It is God's Gospel act reasserting itself in detail . . . It is a sacramental act, done together with the community in the name and power of Christ's redeeming act and our common faith."

Here in Forsyth we have a man who, in a shallow age, was prepared to go deep in his thinking, in his theology, in his preaching. He hits out against the treatment of sin as if it were but lapse, of God's grace as if it were but love, of God's love as if it were but paternal kindness. He insists that God cares more that we should be great than that we should be happy—"we must regain our sense of *soul* greatness, and our sense of its eternal price." He pleads for right priorities in the ministry of preaching—"we must rally at the great strategic forts." What are they? "In the order of importance we should go to the world first of all with the Atoning Cross which is the Alpha and Omega of grace; second, with the resurrection of Christ which is the emergence into experience of the new life won for us on the Cross; third, with the life, character, teaching, and miracles of Christ; fourth, with the pre-existence of Christ, which is a corollary of His Eternal Life. . . ." It would be interesting—humbling, perhaps?—to compare this list of priorities with the average diet given in our pulpits to-day. Is a "re-distribution of emphasis" called for?

Right priorities in preaching! And the great majestic themes! Forsyth jumps in at the deep end. Who to-day preaches predestination? (I am asking a question, not giving an answer, but at least suggesting that many find it too "difficult" and so conveniently by-pass it!) Not so Forsyth. It may be an idea with which most modern preachers feel strangely ill at ease. But is it not written into the warp and woof of our Biblical documents? If we simply by-pass it, are we not jeopardizing the scope and something of the majesty of the message with which we have been entrusted? Are we not reducing the canvas until we have something of the size of a polyphoto—and that not too true to life? Listen to this: "It is easy for any soft humanist or hard witling to hold up to horror or ridicule our fathers' doctrine of predestination, or reprobation. It is easy because we believe in man (if we do) where they believed in God. We are supremely concerned about human happiness where they were engrossed with the glory of God. We are preoccupied with human freedom, and are not interested (as they were above all) in the freedom of God. We are greatly interested in freedom of thought, and little in the freedom of grace; much troubled about freedom of thought or action, and little about freedom of soul."

Let it not be thought that Forsyth was a fundamentalist. Far from it. He has a good deal to say on the benefits of Biblical criticism and the error, as he sees it, of the doctrine of the plenary inspiration of the Bible. But he was one of those great men who seemed to be born before his time—perhaps that is why so many of his books have recently been reprinted, our day being better prepared to receive his teaching than was his own day. He could see through the analysis of documents which was being ruthlessly pursued in his day to that synthesis which we tend to associate more with what is commonly called the post-critical era. He had the insight—and the foresight—of the prophet.

What is Forsyth's message to the preacher of 1961? I single out a few of the things which I believe he would say to us if he were alive to-day—things which stand out clearly in his book and which we as preachers neglect at our peril.

(1) "What is the use of captains who are more at home entertaining the passengers than navigating the ship?" Theology is a greater need than philanthropy—so far as the pulpit is concerned. A theology of experienced grace is not merely of the *bene esse* but of the *esse* of the Church. Without such theology "you have bustle all the week and baldness all the Sunday. You have energy everywhere except in the Spirit". We need fewer homilies upon "Fret not . . ." or "Study to be Quiet . . ." We need more sermons on "Through Him the world is crucified to me and I to the world", or "Him who was made sin for us."

(2) Preachers must be men who do not know the Bible just as a sermon quarry, but who speak from its very interior, as men do who live in it and wonder themselves. The Bible is the one Enchiridion of the preacher still. When that is so, we may expect, as we desperately need, more expository preaching. "Take long passages for texts. Perhaps you have no idea how eager people are to have the Bible expounded, and how much

they prefer you to un-riddle what the Bible says, with its large utterance, than to confuse them with what you can make it say by some ingenuity."

(3) "Do not attempt to heal the hurt of God's people lightly" (Jer. 6:14 and 8:11). "For God's sake do not tell poor prodigals and black scoundrels that they are better than they think, that they have more of Christ in them than they know, and so on. The conscience which is really in hell is the first to be angered at ingenuities and futilities like these, the more exasperating because of the quarter-truth they contain."

The Christian preacher must deal faithfully with human sin. Full of compassion as our Lord was, yet it was not the sorrow of the world that broke His heart, but its wickedness. This will involve—this will include—preaching to *social* sin—the social crisis and demand cannot be ignored. But it must be remarked that that will involve knowing the ethic of the gospel on the one hand, and the economics of the age on the other. That is to make big demands on the preacher, but, then, preaching is a demanding thing!

(4) What about the preacher's own doubts, his own unresolved strivings with truth? "He is a minister of the Gospel, not a professor of scientific theology. There are truths we must say to all, and truths we should say to some; and there are truths we can only tell to those who ask. It is not the preacher's duty to tell everything he knows about the Bible; but it is his duty to tell everything he knows about the Gospel, and in this reduced yet enlarged sense . . . to declare the whole counsel of God."

(5) What about those who are impatient of the sermon, who demand brevity before everything else? Forsyth's word is stern. "Those who say they want little sermon because they are there to worship God and not hear man, have not grasped the rudiments of the first idea of Christian worship. . . . A Christianity of short sermons is a Christianity of short fibre."

With the insight of a true prophet, Forsyth put his finger on three things from which the Church of his day suffered. They were triviality (externality), uncertainty of its foundation, and satisfaction with itself. For *triviality*, he prescribed a new note of greatness in our creed, the note that sounds in a theology more than in a sentiment. For *uncertainty*, he prescribed a new note of wrestling and reality in prayer. For *complacency*, he prescribed a new note of judgment in our salvation.

That was in 1907. Is the diagnosis far out for 1961, or, for that matter, the prescription?

It is greatly to be desired that this book should be widely re-read. And with this in view, we are glad to learn that it has been re-printed by the Independent Press. One of the greatest needs of the Church of the 1960's is a revival of its preaching ministry. A study of this book would make no small contribution to that end.

18

MUTED NOTES IN MODERN PREACHING

From *The Church of England Newspaper*, November 25th, 1960

18

IS MODERN PREACHING teaching men to *die*? That is not a
morbid question. It is simply another way of asking: Have
the horizons of modern preaching shrunk to narrower limits
than those of the Biblical revelation? Or, to put it another way:
Have we reacted so violently against an aberration of an earlier
age, that to-day our preaching is almost entirely *this*-worldly?
These questions are of immense importance, and, particularly,
demand an answer from clergy and indeed from all who preach
and teach the Christian faith.

It is easy and it is natural to react. Some of us were brought
up on hymns which gave the impression that the chief desire of
those who sang them was to be wafted from this vale of tears
to the streets of gold with as little delay as possible. The hymns
were sometimes supported by a theology illustrated by charts
of the End whose chronological details were scarcely justified
by the Biblical revelation! We smile. We murmur: "Very
crude." But that is an easy course to take. It is like the attitude
of a man who says, "Because the book of the Revelation has
been the happy hunting-ground of so many religious cranks and
fanatics, I will not touch it nor preach from it." He thus leaves
a large part of the Bible undealt with and unwrestled with,
and he and his congregation are the poorer.

It is easy to preach a this-worldly religion only. But to do so
is to be traitors to our people, and to the "deposit" committed
to our charge. Indeed, the power of Christianity derives in
large part from the fact that it is a this-worldly religion *and* an
other-worldly religion. Its music is made by the tautness of the
string one end of which is in this world and the other in that.
Relax that tension, and the power and the music go. It is
strange how little is said in the Church Catechism on the matter
of the world to come, and it is the hope of the revisers that, at
least to some extent, that mistake may be remedied.

Anyone who aspires to preach to-day must surely ask himself

whether he has some kind of Christian philosophy of history, and whether he has something clear to say about the End. The Communist, concerned as he is with this world, has a philosophy of history even though it be an atheistic one. What is the Christian to say? Must he, with H. A. L. Fisher, confess that he can trace no design or pattern? Or may he, with K. S. Latourette and Herbert Butterfield, see in history at least the outskirts of God's ways?

It is my conviction that we need to get back to the New Testament concept of God as the Lord of history, and to preach this with vigour. A renewed study of the book of Revelation would help us in this respect. And a renewed study of the Christian doctrine of *hope* (that much neglected member of the trio, faith, hope and love) would surely reveal that its power derives from the profound belief that the God who has set His hand to the plough will never look back however menacing the forces of sin may appear to be. Helmut Thielicke, the dean of the Faculty of Theology in the University of Hamburg, has put it well:

> The one thing above all that we are saying is that history will surely arrive at its goal. We receive a message that tells us there is Another who determines this goal, because in his time he will be there, because he will appear on the horizon of the world . . . One is coming to us from the other side and . . . the world's history will end at his feet . . . He has told us that at the close the Victor alone will be left upon the battlefield and that on the horizon of our little lives and also on the horizon of history itself there stands One at whose feet all the zigzag, circuitous roads of existence will end. Even my little life, lived in this Advent certainty, is an adventure . . .

I ask—is this a muted note, or a trumpet note, in modern preaching?

Again, there is no doubt that in New Testament times the belief that all were one day to stand before the judgment seat of Christ was not a barren item of eschatological belief but a most potent factor in ethics and conduct. The ordinary happenings of everyday life assumed a deep significance if it was believed (as it undoubtedly was) that an account would be given for the deeds done in the body. There was no morbidity about this belief, nor was there fear, for "perfect love casts out fear". But the holding of that belief added a seriousness, a purposefulness to life of which those who did not hold it knew nothing. There can be no flippancy in regard to this life if you believe *that* about its consummation.

"As he reasoned of righteousness, temperance, and judgment to come, Felix trembled" (Acts 24: 25). Small wonder. Felix's life was not a very savoury one. And there was that about St. Paul's preaching which carried its own conviction with it. You might prevaricate; you might procrastinate—Felix was good at doing that. But suppose that what Paul said were *true* . . . ?

I ask again—is this a muted note, or a trumpet note, in modern preaching? If it be true that by and large it has been over the last decade or two a muted note, is it possible that the state of moral chaos which prevails in England to-day must be in part laid to the charge of us who have preached a feeble doctrine of judgment to come? Is it not true that to many of us preaching on Advent Sunday has been as difficult as preaching on Whit Sunday or—even worse—Trinity Sunday? So we have lapsed into little this-worldly homilies. So we have limited the horizons of our Gospel. So our young people have hardly heard of judgment to come, of an account to be rendered, of a great white throne.

I am not pleading for a return to a message of threatening and fear. God forbid. I am asking whether the preachers and teachers of the Church are blameless in regard to the state of moral chaos in which we are sunk to-day. I am asking whether you can have great morals without great doctrine.

The essence of the Advent hope, of Christian eschatology, so it seems to me, is not to be found in an elaborate scheme of events which can be delineated on a chart. Rather, it is summed up by St. John in his first Epistle: "Beloved, we are God's children now; it does not yet appear what we shall be, but we know that when He appears we shall be like Him, for we shall see Him as He is" (R.S.V.). *That,* to the early Christians, was the *eschaton.* He, the crucified, risen, glorified One was Lord of history and Lord of their lives. He was the One

ever to be worshipped.
Trusted, and adored,

He would appear, His enemies finally defeated. They who had been "in Him" here would be "with Him" there. That was their unshakable hope, their never-dying conviction. With that within them, they reigned as kings even while they were persecuted as traitors to all that the world held dearest.

In (their) hands
The thing became a trumpet, whence (they) blew
Soul-animating strains.

A muted note? A trumpet sound? Which?

19

"GIVE ATTENDANCE TO READING"

From *The Church Times* Book Supplement, November 24, 1961

19

ONE OF THE enjoyable things about the study of Holy Scripture is that there are so many incidents and passages which, having been read over and yielded good sense, seem to beckon the reader and say to him: "Look again. Are you sure that what you have seen is all that there is to see? Is there not another meaning, which so far you have not glimpsed?" This happens also in relation to single phrases or words. I am thinking now particularly of the word "reading", in the exhortation in 1 Timothy 4:13 "Give attendance to reading." What does reading mean? Public reading of Scripture? Or private reading? Or both?

"Concentrate . . . on your reading," says J. B. Phillips, non-committally following the lead of the Authorized Version "Attend to your Scripture reading," says Moffatt, in a phrase which, by itself, might refer to public or private reading. "Attend to the public reading of Scripture," says the Revised Standard Version.

You can tell the character of a man by the kind of company he keeps. You can often tell the meaning of a word by the words which act as near companions to it. In this case the words are "exhortation" and "doctrine" (teaching). It would seem, then, that the writer of the Epistle had in mind public reading in the worship of the Church. And, indeed, the word is so used in Acts 13:15 and 2 Cor. 3:14.

Would to God that this injunction were heeded in all the churches of the land! Would to God that, every Saturday night, clergy, lay readers, churchwardens and all those who have the priceless privilege of reading the lessons were found *giving attention to the reading* which they will do in God's name next day. This is work of the very greatest importance, calling for dedication, prayer, intelligent understanding, and preparation both of the passages to be read and of the person who is to read them. This it is which makes the difference between dull monotony and a moving experience in which God is found to be speaking to His people.

"Give attention to the public reading of Scripture"—that, I doubt not, is the meaning of the phrase in its original context. But may we not legitimately look again at the phrase, and hear it bid us give care to *reading* in a wider but less public sense? Indeed, anyone, clerical or lay, who is to engage in "exhortation and doctrine" will find such a ministry getting very thin and anaemic unless behind that ministry there is very careful "attention to reading". A well-stored mind, nourished on well-furnished bookshelves, will result in exhortation and doctrine which are never arid, never listless, never dull. The problem of how to fill up twenty minutes next Sunday is never so acute for a man who is well-read as it is for the man who has allowed his attention to reading to lapse. But if preaching is to be fresh, two ingredients at least must go to the maintenance of that freshness. One is a deep love for the Master. The other is good, solid, down-to-earth attention to reading.

But I cannot leave the matter there. Here, in this injunction, I believe, we touch an obligation which is incumbent on *all* Christians who are reasonably educated. I do not say that God's grace comes only through the intellect. That is obviously untrue. But I do say that one avenue of God's grace is all too often obstructed because we allow our minds to stagnate and fail to exercise them by grappling with good books. "Thou shalt love the Lord thy God with all thy . . . mind" is a command which, if neglected, results all too soon in listlessness and in a discipleship blunted in its cutting edge.

The temptations to neglect reading are legion. It is, of course, easier to sit and watch something being done for you through the medium of television than it is to dig the heart out of a book or to come to terms with some great central doctrine of the faith. That calls for concentration. But such concentration equips the man of God for service and for battle. And it is men of God of *that* calibre who are needed if the Christian faith is to be commended to those who now are unpersuaded of its truth.

Never before, I think, has it been so easy for a Christian to obey the injunction "give attendance to reading" as it is to-day. Working hours for the average man are shorter than in years gone by, leaving longer hours for leisure. One of the really important questions which every dedicated Christian must ask —and to which he must work out an answer—is : "How do I in the sight of God use my leisure time?" It would not be a bad idea to answer that question, as in the presence of God, with pen and paper before me. A bit of honest work, as a survey is made of the working hours of the day, might yield some surprising results.

From another point of view, the way is made easy for us to "give attendance to reading". If you are thinking of the private reading and study of the Bible, there are available all kinds of guides for people at all stages of growth. (One thinks, e.g. of the widely varied series of notes put out by the Bible Reading Fellowship.) And no one need be hindered in his study of the Bible by working on a version which is antiquated and unattractive. But if you are thinking of reading in wider terms, I think it is safe to say that never before has there been so wide a range of books available in cheap editions as there is to-day.

20

"I MAKE ALL THINGS NEW"

He that sat upon the throne said, Behold, I make all things new (Revelation 21 : 5)
The Son of Man is come to seek and to save that which was lost (St. Luke 19 : 10)

A sermon preached in Coventry Cathedral on Saturday, May 26, 1962, at the first Eucharist after the consecration of the Cathedral on May 25

20

WHAT WORDS COULD express more adequately and simply the essence of all that is in our hearts and minds to-day than the words with which the Epistle this morning ended: "He that sat upon the throne said, Behold, I make all things new"? Out of chaos, this lovely thing has risen; out of destruction wrought by man's hatred of man has come this centre of love and unity; out of the desolation of the old has emerged the splendour of the new.

This Cathedral Church of St. Michael, Coventry, is a symbol in stone and glass of what the seer wrote about in his vision—the day when there would be "no more death, neither sorrow, nor crying, neither shall there be any more pain: for the former things are passed away". The Precentor has aptly described a Cathedral as "a doxology—an enthusiastic gesture of love and obedience to God". Such indeed this Cathedral is.

If the Epistle lifted our eyes to God on His throne and pointed us forward to the day when all would be made new, the Gospel brought us down to earth with a vengeance. The passage was concerned with a *little* man—little in every way. He was little in stature—he could not help that. But he was little in soul—his horizons did not seem to stretch beyond the business of getting money; and he was not over-scrupulous as to how he got it. And then he came into touch with Jesus. That contact made him see, with a kind of blinding clarity, the sordidness, the emptiness, of a life lived in money-grubbing, a life lived apart from the life of God and without love for his neighbours. That contact with Jesus wrought a revolution in Zacchaeus' soul. "Here and now, sir," he said to Jesus, "I give half my possessions to charity; and if I have cheated any-one, I am ready to pay him four times over." There was a note of jubilation in the Master's reply: "Salvation has come to this house to-day—the Son of Man has come to seek and save what was lost." Zacchaeus' wreck of a soul had been remade. "Behold, I make all things new." Our Lord's jubilation was centred, not just in a generous act undertaken by Zacchaeus. Rather, He saw that act as an outward and visible sign of a renewal within. The spiritual life of Zacchaeus, stunted, starved, ruined hitherto, was now free to grow. He was in process of being remade, renewed, fashioned after the pattern of Christ.

On one of the walls of my chapel at Bishopthorpe, York, is a tablet. It records how Archbishop Maclagan, in the year 1892, "to the glory of God made anew and beautified" a chapel which for many years had been defaced and in bad repair. "Made anew and beautified"—that is an apt description of what we see around us to-day: "Beauty for ashes, the oil of joy for mourning, the garment of praise for the spirit of heaviness." This first Eucharist in this Cathedral is its thanskgiving for its renewal and beautifying.

> Small it is, in this poor sort
> To enrol Thee;

nevertheless, as best we can, and all unworthily, we proffer for God's acceptance "craftsman's art and music's measure", and we know it will not be refused.

All this, however—all this splendour of music and colour and skill—points to other offerings unseen by any eyes but God's. There are hearts of men and women in this Cathedral this morning, hearts marred and spoilt by the ravages of sin, of passion, of greed, or of long-nourished hate; *little* men, stunted and starved like Zacchaeus, whom Christ wants to seek and to save as He sought and saved him; whom God wants to release, to "make anew and beautify" by the power of His Spirit. "He that sat on the throne said, Behold, I make all things new."

This re-creative work of God is pin-pointed in this very service of Holy Communion. Who are invited to share in the bread broken and the wine outpoured? Those who "intend to lead a *new* life". This is not turning over some new leaf. This is committal to Him who alone can make us anew, as He re-made and beautified Zacchaeus. This is abandonment of self to Him who alone can forgive, and in whose power alone we can "serve and please" God "in newness of life".

The Holy Communion service bids us look far beyond the confines of this lovely place, to a world torn by hatred and suspicion, much of it maimed by poverty and near-starvation, a large part of its population stunted in their development, illiterate and without the light of Christian faith. The Son of Man has come to seek and to save such as these, just as truly as He came to seek and to save us who happen to have been born in the West or in this favoured island. Those who are nourished by the Body and Blood of Christ are nourished for battle, for service, for the spreading of the light which has illuminated them. The bread and the wine are not luxuries for those who are prepared merely to loiter by the way. They are warriors' food, preparing Christian men and women to go into battle.

Here, it seems to me, is a matter of primary importance for England to-day—for its leaders in the realm of politics and industry and thought, and for the great majority who never get into the limelight but who constitute the backbone of our nation. Comparatively speaking, very few of our people would call themselves atheists, though more might answer to the label of agnostic. Comparatively few of us, on the other hand, are unshakably convinced Christians, the sort who would go on being Christian if that involved them in danger or ignominy or social ostracism. Between these two classes—the atheists and the out-and-out Christians—comes a vast company of men and women who like a little religion on great occasions, great moments in personal or family life, great occasions of Church or State, and who pay lip-service to "Christian principles" and to the "Sermon on the Mount"; but that is all. Of the joy of being made anew and beautified by the Spirit of God, of allowing themselves to be sought and saved by the Son of Man who is the risen Son of God, of this they know nothing. And, as a consequence, they miss the wonder of being what every baptized member of Christ is meant to be, an agent of the living God, co-operating with Him in the remaking and beautifying of others.

This is a service of offering. We offer the best we have of art and craft and music and needlework. We offer our gifts of money for the completion of this building. We offer the bread and the wine as tokens of our toil. And David's challenge to his people, when he commended to them his son Solomon for the building of the Temple, comes ringing down the years to us: "Who then will offer willingly, consecrating *himself—to-day*—to the Lord?"

In truth, we have nothing to offer of our own, for He has given us all—nothing to offer but our sin, from which we would fain be delivered. And God in Christ has everything to offer us —freedom from the old bondage; renewal and beautifying by the power of His Spirit; a task to do for Him in a world still beset by sin and hate and sorrow.

He *summons* us—"Come, follow Me."
He *calls* us—"Let us go together to reclaim the lost."
He *enables us*—"Here is food for the journey and for the battle; bread of life and wine of joy. Bread of the world in mercy broken; wine of the soul in mercy shed. Come: take, eat, and live."

"Lift up your hearts!" What a day for dedication!—the past behind us, forgiven and blotted out; the future before us, big with opportunities to serve our Lord and His needy ones; the present, ours to look up and say, with full hearts and dedicated wills: "We are not worthy. But Thou art the same Lord, whose property is always to forgive. Here we offer and present ourselves, our souls and bodies . . . unto Thee."

"Lift up your hearts!" We lift them, Lord, to Thee;
Here at Thy feet none other may we see:
"Lift up your hearts!" E'en so, with one accord,
We lift them up, we lift them to the Lord.

Above the level of the former years,
The mire of sin, the slough of guilty fears,
The mist of doubt, the blight of love's decay,
O Lord of Light, lift all our hearts to-day!

Lift every gift that Thou Thyself hast given;
Low lies the best till lifted up to heaven:
Low lie the bounding heart, the teeming brain,
Till, sent from God, they mount to God again.

Then, as the trumpet-call in after years,
"Lift up your hearts!" rings pealing in our ears,
Still shall those hearts respond with full accord,
"We lift them up, we lift them to the Lord!"